STEDELIJK MUSEUM AMSTERDAM

COLLECTION GUIDE

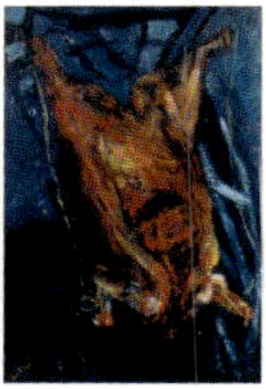

e

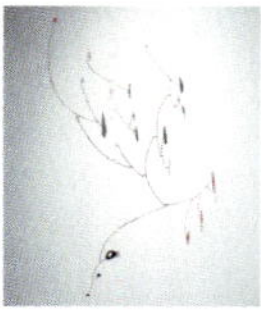

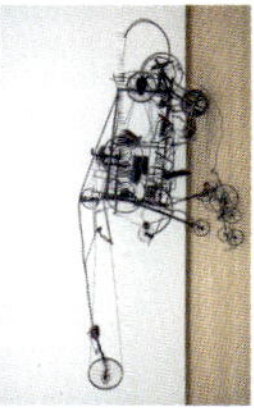

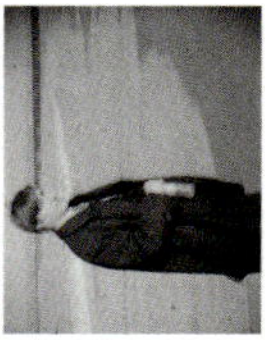

PREFACE

Everyone can discover and experience art at the Stedelijk Museum Amsterdam. Art shows us who we are, and how we relate to the world around us. It also shows us how the world is changing – sometimes right in front of our eyes, sometimes behind our backs. Artists question the past, present, and future, and the Stedelijk collects and displays their work. Our aim is to better understand the present through art and design.

The Stedelijk Museum has therefore always been a place for experimentation. From the first solo exhibition by Vincent van Gogh in the Netherlands (1905) to 365 consecutive days of live art during Tino Sehgal's *A Year at the Stedelijk* (2015). From the space-age fashion show featuring the unconventional jewelry of Emmy van Leersum and Gijs Bakker (1967) to table tennis on the Museumplein with Rirkrit Tiravanija (2016).

This urge to experiment also means every visit to the Stedelijk Museum is a surprise, and that everyone who comes to see art here – even the most seasoned, well-read visitor – sometimes asks, "What am I actually looking at?" or "What exactly is happening here?" or even "What am I expected to do?"

A guide that gives a little extra background information can be very helpful on such occasions.

YOUR GUIDE

This publication tells readers more about many beautiful, extraordinary, and relatively unknown works of art, and about the unique history of this museum. If you want to learn more about abstract art, expressionism, or "appropriation art," simply turn to the essays in the back. And if you're not sure exactly what appropriation art is, you can consult the list of terminology found on the cover flaps. Back at home, settled comfortably on the couch, you can relive your visit while browsing through this book.

We have selected one hundred works of art from the Stedelijk's collection and ordered them chronologically. As a result, all kinds of art (paintings, sculptures, photographs, chairs, drawings, ball pits, etc.) are jumbled together. The Stedelijk Museum considers the collection as a single entity – each work belongs to the time in which it was made. Leafing through the book from front to back, you will see how art changes over the years. By presenting different disciplines alongside each other, we can learn more about a period, and perhaps even identify new connections. In the back of the book are ten essays that explore in greater depth how art has changed over the past 150 years. Moreover, we have included the occasional photograph of the galleries, showing that it is not only art that is in constant motion – the Stedelijk Museum itself is, too.

We wish you, the reader, many enjoyable hours with this book.

Stedelijk Museum Amsterdam

Exhibition *Rondom Rodin* (About Rodin), 1939

AUGUSTE RODIN
1840, Paris – 1917, Meudon (FR)
Jean d'Aire, 1884–1886 (date of casting unknown)
Patinated bronze, 203.5 × 75 × 67 cm

Auguste Rodin could bring stone to life. The men and women he depicted in his large, unfinished sculptures have clear emotions and appear to move. Rodin believed that modern art should express suffering and conflict. *Jean d'Aire* is a magnificent portrayal of suffering, a piece full of repressed tension and despair. The facial expression, wide stance, and curling toes are testament to the man's tenacity. This is one of six figures from Rodin's famous *Burghers of Calais*, which depicts an event of 1347, during the Hundred Years' War. Jean d'Aire has the keys to the town of Calais in his hands, and is about to set out with four fellow townsmen for the enemy English camp, all with nooses around their necks. Each man is prepared to die in order to end the eleven-month siege of the town. Rodin chose to depict this historical event as a human drama in which each of the six men reacts in his own way. This makes the six figures so powerful and expressive that they can easily stand as individual sculptures.

Philippa of Hainault was, incidentally, so moved by the plea of the six men that she begged her husband, King Edward III of England, to spare them, and he agreed.

PAUL CÉZANNE
1839–1906, Aix-en-Provence (FR)
La Montagne Sainte-Victoire, ca. 1888
Oil on canvas, 54 × 65 cm, gift of the Association for the Formation of a Public Collection of Contemporary Art in Amsterdam (VVHK), 1949

Like the impressionists, Paul Cézanne was obsessed by observation. But unlike Claude Monet, for example, who attempted to capture constantly changing moments in series of paintings, Cézanne was interested in timelessness. He sought the structure underlying all things, attempting to reduce forms that occur in nature, from apples to mountain landscapes, to their geometric essence in his paintings. He also set out to give the flat surface of the painting the illusion of depth and to create volumes using color. Besides still lifes, the many faces of Montagne Sainte-Victoire are another focus of his work. From 1882 onwards he painted this limestone mountain ridge in Provence at least fifty times. The feature that typifies these landscapes lies in the point at which Cézanne deemed them to be finished: not when the canvas was full, but when he felt he had achieved the most he could in the painting. When Émile Bernard, a painter with whom Cézanne corresponded frequently, reminded him that line, composition, and light were essential elements of painting for classical artists, he replied, "They make pictures; we are trying to create a piece of nature." Cézanne's indefatigable attempts to capture primitive forms paved the way for cubism, and thereby also modern art.

The Van Gogh room at the Stedelijk, 1934

VINCENT VAN GOGH
1853, Zundert (NL) – 1890, Auvers-sur-Oise (FR)
Augustine Roulin (La Berceuse) (Augustine Roulin [Woman Rocking a Cradle]), 1889
Oil on canvas, 92 × 72.5 cm, gift of V.W. van Gogh, Laren (NL), 1945

Vincent van Gogh's brightly colored and emotionally charged paintings are among the most famous artworks created in the nineteenth century. Although Van Gogh did not belong to any particular movement or group, his use of color, brushwork, and symbolic expression formed the basis for later movements like fauvism and expressionism.

Van Gogh's landscapes have attracted particular praise, but the artist himself preferred to paint portraits. In a letter to his sister, he explained how he sought to express and intensify the sitter's personality using color. In Arles, Van Gogh painted a whole series of portraits of his friend, the postman Joseph Roulin, and his wife, Augustine. Influenced by Japanese prints, he painted a two-dimensional portrait of Augustine. Devoid of depth, the solid shapes and flower motifs appear detached from reality.

He called this maternal image of Augustine *La Berceuse*, or *Woman Rocking a Cradle*. In a small sketch in one of the hundreds of letters he sent to his brother, Theo, Van Gogh placed her at the center of a triptych with sunflowers on either side. He predicted that the yellow and orange tones on her head would gain more resonance thanks to the yellow panels beside them. The Stedelijk would like to recreate this envisaged triptych, but unfortunately has only one of Van Gogh's *Sunflowers* paintings in its collection.

GEORGE HENDRIK BREITNER
1857, Rotterdam – 1923, Amsterdam (NL)
The Red Kimono, ca. 1893–1894
Oil on canvas, 51.5 × 76 cm, gift of the Association for the Formation of a Public Collection of Contemporary Art in Amsterdam (VVHK), 1949

When George Hendrik Breitner saw an exhibition of Japanese prints in The Hague, he immediately went out and bought several kimonos. Using a screen, divan, and rugs, he created an oriental atmosphere in his studio. He then invited his neighbors, Anna and Geesje Kwak, to model for him. Geesje appears most frequently in the paintings of girls in kimono, and in the associated photographs and sketches that Breitner produced in 1893 and 1894. *The Red Kimono* is one of the best examples of Breitner's way with forms, colors, and textures. He even used a comb to imitate the fabric of the thick rug.
The photographs he took and the rapid sketches he made also enabled Breitner to record late nineteenth-century Amsterdam. No other painter ever depicted the bustle of the rapidly growing city so directly and vividly as Breitner. Demolition and construction work, trams, horses, people passing through the image: Breitner's impressionistic city scenes are full of movement, and form a stark contrast to the peace and intimacy of the demure paintings of girls in kimono.

HENDRIK PETRUS BERLAGE
1856, Amsterdam – 1934, The Hague (NL)
Wall Clock, 1904 (design)
Manufactured by Becht & Dijserinck, Amsterdam, brass, copper alloy, iron, paint, 58 × 34.5 × 12 cm, gift of G.D.H. Stibbe, Oisterwijk and E. Stibbe, Bergeijk (NL), 1978

This clock will not have been to everyone's taste in the early twentieth century. Its understated design was unprecedented. But to the designer, architect H.P. Berlage, the clock was the perfect example of an honest product. For Berlage, "honest" meant a clear structure, logical use of materials, restrained decoration, and affordable. The clock was sold at Verkooplokaal 't Binnenhuis, which Berlage and several like-minded designers had established as a response to what they regarded as the worthless products on sale at existing home furnishing stores. The store sold both individual items and complete interiors. Berlage regarded harmony as highly important. The interior and exterior of a building must form a single whole. His own house in The Hague exemplified this ideal. He had designed the lamps, heating stove, furniture, and even the cutlery himself. The best-known and most universally accessible examples of Berlage's *Gesamtkunstwerke* are the Gemeentemuseum in The Hague and the Amsterdam Commodity Exchange, better known as the Beurs van Berlage (1896–1903). Berlage attempted to create a better and more beautiful world in his architecture. In the spirit of socialism, he was convinced that art and architecture could help achieve such a world.

Collection presentation, 1995

ERNST LUDWIG KIRCHNER
1880, Aschaffenburg (DE) – 1938, Davos (CH)
Tanzende (Dancing Woman), 1911
Painted alder wood, 87 × 35.5 × 27.5 cm

"Whoever renders directly and authentically that which impels him to create is one of us," Ernst Ludwig Kirchner wrote in 1906, in the manifesto of Die Brücke ("The Bridge"), a group of expressionist artists from Dresden. He used bright colors and angular shapes to depict life in the city and summer leisure at the lakes nearby. His own studio also provided a backdrop for his paintings, drawings, and woodcuts.

Kirchner was a great admirer of Henri Matisse (p. 85) and Vincent van Gogh (p. 15), and also of primitive art, which he saw at the Museum of Ethnology in Dresden. Carvings from Africa and the Pacific inspired him to seek the same immediacy in his own work. *Tanzende* closely resembles a figure of a Bangwa queen acquired just before 1900 by the Museum für Völkerkunde in Berlin.

The dancing woman was one of his earliest sculptures. She is carved from alder, her shape determined by the tree trunk, which Kirchner first worked with an axe, and then a knife. To make the sculpture even more expressive, he decided to paint the rough surface. The shape, color, and movement combine to suggest that *Tanzende* has just stepped out of one of Kirchner's paintings and assumed three-dimensional form.

Exhibition *Chagall: 75 drawings*, 1956

MARC CHAGALL
1887, Vitebsk (BY) – 1985, Saint-Paul-de-Vence (FR)
L'autoportrait aux sept doigts (Self-Portrait with Seven Fingers), 1912–1913
Oil on canvas, 126 × 107 cm, on loan from the Netherlands Cultural Heritage Agency, 1953

Marc Chagall had his heyday in Paris in the early twentieth century. *Self-Portrait with Seven Fingers* shows how he developed his own unique style using the bright colors of the fauvists and the geometric forms of the cubists. The red wall and his angular self-portrait are reminiscent of the works of contemporaries like Picasso (p. 91), but the fairytale atmosphere and references to Hassidic Jewish culture are typical of Chagall. Logic plays no role in his symbolic images.
In this self-portrait, Chagall depicts himself as an artist caught between two worlds. The window affords a view of both the Eiffel Tower and, in the clouds, a small village with a Russian Orthodox church, a reference to the village near Vitebsk where Chagall was born. The seven fingers on his left hand also refer to Jewish tradition, in which the number seven has mystical meaning. However successful and cosmopolitan Chagall was to become, the Russian folk art of his childhood and his Hassidic Jewish roots always remained a rich source of inspiration for him. The Stedelijk Museum has a large number of works by Chagall in its collection, including *Maternité* and the famous *Le violoniste,* both of which date from the same period as *Self-Portrait with Seven Fingers.*

WASSILY KANDINSKY
1866, Moscow (RU) – 1944, Neuilly-sur-Seine (FR)
Improvisation 33 (Orient I), 1913
Oil on canvas, 88.5 × 100.5 cm

Wassily Kandinsky was one of the pioneers who sought to penetrate the essence of art by abandoning the representation of visible reality. With visual elements pared down to their spiritual core, the Russian painter set out to penetrate the very soul of his audience in the way that music can. "How lucky musicians are with such a progressive art!" Kandinsky wrote to composer Arnold Schönberg in 1911. Inspired by his admiration for the spiritual power and abstract nature of music, Kandinsky gave his paintings titles derived from music, such as "composition" and "improvisation." *Improvisation 33 (Orient I)* is one of his first abstract works. Radiant, intermingling patches of color create a space in which lines take on a life of their own, free of form and color. It looks spontaneous, but the composition was in fact carefully prepared in sketches and watercolors. If one holds the preliminary studies beside the finished work, the shapes of a minaret, a fountain and, in the foreground, a recumbent woman and standing figure can still be vaguely discerned in the lines and patches of color.

KARL SCHMIDT-ROTTLUFF
1884, Rottluff – 1976, Berlin (DE)
Kopf mit Halskette (Head with Necklace), 1914
Woodcut, 35.9 × 29.2 cm, gift heirs Dr. Rosa Schapiro, London (GB), 1956

Karl Schmidt-Rottluff was one of the founders of the German expressionist group Die Brücke ("The Bridge"), together with Ernst Ludwig Kirchner, Fritz Bleyl, and Schmidt-Rottluff's childhood friend, Erich Heckel. Together they renounced the dominant academic style and sought to embrace the new art that was coming out of Paris, fauvism, without throwing away their national cultural heritage, thereby forming a bridge between the past and the present. They developed a style with vivid colors and strong lines that included a marked influence of sculptures and masks from Africa and Oceania. Their aim was not to represent reality, but rather the emotions it raises.
Schmidt-Rottluff and the other artists of Die Brücke worked in all kinds of media: they painted, made sculptures, and produced graphic work. But the medium that connected the new art to the grand tradition of Cranach and Dürer was the woodblock print, and it was this technique that dominated Schmidt-Rottluff's printed work from approximately 1909 to 1920.
In this striking woodcut print, *Kopf mit Halskette,* the angular depiction of the woman's face recalls both cubist techniques and the influence of African sculpture, a style which had captured the attention of many modernists in the first decades of the twentieth century, including Pablo Picasso (p. 91), Henri Matisse (p. 85), and the German expressionists.

Collection presentation, 2012

KAZIMIR MALEVICH
1879, Kiev (UA) – 1935, Leningrad (RU)
Suprematist Composition (with Eight Red Rectangles), 1915
Oil on canvas, 58 × 48.5 cm, ownership recognized by agreement with the Estate of Kazimir Malevich in 2008

Kazimir Malevich, obsessed with movement, attempted to capture energy and dynamics on the canvas. *Suprematist Composition (with Eight Red Rectangles)* was one of his first "objectless" paintings. The red rectangles are not merely flat shapes on a white canvass, but eight bodies with both mass and direction, which the painter captured as they traveled endlessly through space and time. Never before had an artist so radically departed from visual reality and all previous ideas about color, form, and perspective. Malevich regarded abstract, purely pictorial paintings as superior, which is why he called his new style "suprematism."
Before Malevich began to work in an abstract style, he produced figurative paintings featuring a mix of folklore, primitivism, and modernity. When German architect Hugo Häring invited him to exhibit work in Berlin in 1927, he hung his suprematist paintings alongside a number of earlier works, including *An Englishman in Moscow* and *The Woodcutter*. After the exhibition he gave the pieces to Häring for safekeeping, so they survived the war. In 1958, during the directorship of Willem Sandberg, Häring's widow Roma Bahn sold twenty-nine paintings to the Amsterdam city council, which is why the Stedelijk has the most important Malevich collection outside of Russia.

LAMBERTUS ZWIERS
1871, Oldemarkt – 1953, Voorburg (NL)
Wallpaper, 1916–1917
Relief print, 274.5 × 61.3 cm

In 1917 the Stedelijk hosted a solo exhibition of the work of well-known Dutch architect Lambertus Zwiers. Rather than architectural designs, however, Zwiers displayed a series of applied arts, including printed fabrics and wallpaper designs, as a result of his lack of architectural commissions during wartime. Zwiers used intense colors in these designs: flaming red, burning orange, luminous green and bright yellow in combination with black, dark purple, white and gilding. Zwiers had spent some time working in the Dutch East Indies, which certainly influenced his work, although his palette probably owes more to expressionist painting. This design is a very early example of the style of the Amsterdam School.

The Amsterdam School was the Dutch variant of art nouveau, the international movement that arose at the end of the nineteenth century, when designers rejected the use of historical styles in pursuit of contemporary forms. This same urge to create something new sparked the emergence of the Amsterdam School between 1910 and 1915. Its influence was felt in every area of design, from furniture to jewelry, textiles, and graphic design.

CHAÏM SOUTINE
1893, Smilavichy (BY) – 1943, Paris (FR)
Le boeuf (The Beef), ca. 1925
Oil on canvas, 166 × 115 cm

Chaïm Soutine, who came from a Lithuanian-Jewish family of tailors, arrived in Paris in 1913. He would produce this monumental painting there ten years later. It was inspired by Rembrandt's *Slaughtered Ox*, which Soutine had seen in the Louvre, where he had been struck by the artist's bold mastery of paint. To equal that intensity, he had a slaughtered ox brought to his studio and painted as many versions of the carcass as he could, without stopping to rest, until it began to stink so unbearably that the police came to remove it. Rembrandt's ox (ca. 1640) hangs in a cowshed, but Soutine gets much closer to the animal. Everything about the painting reflects his fascination with the different hues and the structure of bones and flesh. Several layers of color can be glimpsed through the thick paint surface. The asymmetrical positioning of the carcass against a royal blue background gives the image even more drama. Soutine does two things here: he confronts the viewer with death and decay, and demonstrates artistic freedom and an intensity of painting that would leave a great impression on later generations of artists. As Soutine looked to Rembrandt, so Jackson Pollock, Francis Bacon, and Georg Baselitz (p. 39) looked to Soutine.

e
r

HENDRIK NICOLAAS WERKMAN
1882, Leens – 1945, Bakkeveen (NL)
The Next Call I, 1926
Hand press on paper, 27.4 × 21.5 cm, gift of C.H. Spruit, Huis ter Heide (NL), 1961

Hendrik Werkman printed books, founded and published several journals, and was a member of the Groningen artists' association De Ploeg ("The Plough"). He also wrote experimental poetry and stories, and was a member of the Dutch resistance during the German occupation. This graphic artist liked to work with whatever was at hand. "Art is everywhere," he wrote in 1923. "It lands on people as if dropped by the birds." In his case, "everywhere" was the attic of a warehouse in Groningen, where he took an experimental approach to printing books. His images were created by improvisation, often using multiple layers of print. For the cover of the first issue of the journal *The Next Call* he used the side of a large letter, a blank space, and a piece of card. Werkman's best-known works, however, are the colorful illustrations for an edition of *Hassidic Legends*, which he printed during the occupation for the clandestine publishing collective De Blauwe Schuit, where he played a key role in his capacity as printer. Werkman was arrested in March 1945 on suspicion of printing illegal material and was executed by firing squad in Friesland three days before the liberation of the northern Netherlands.

Exhibition *Gerrit Rietveld*, 1971

GERRIT RIETVELD AND TRUUS SCHRÖDER-SCHRÄDER
Rietveld: 1888–1964, Utrecht (NL)
Schröder-Schräder: 1889, Deventer – 1985, Utrecht (NL)
Harrenstein slaapkamer, 1926
Produced under the control of Gerrit Rietveld, Utrecht (NL), bedroom furniture, wood, board, glass, mirrored glass, metal, porcelain, paint; dimensions: 303 × 508 × 591 cm

The bedroom that Gerrit Rietveld designed for Amsterdam pediatrician Rein Harrenstein and his wife, An Harrenstein-Schräder, consists of fifteen partially integrated items of furniture and colored rectangular planes that divide the space. It is one of the few surviving original interiors from the De Stijl-period.
The couple's home was a hub of the avant-garde art scene. They came into contact with Rietveld through An's sister, Truus Schröder-Schräder, for whom he had designed the world-famous Rietveld-Schröder House in Utrecht, completed in 1924. Rietveld and Truus designed the bedroom together, and were also commissioned to furnish other rooms in the house. Nothing remains of those designs, however, except for a few individual pieces of furniture and photographs.
The Stedelijk Museum acquired the *Harrenstein Bedroom* in 1971. Since the interior includes both furniture and some interventions in the physical space, including a layered ceiling lit from above, a casing has been specially made in the original dimensions of the room. Visitors can view the interior through the windows and doors.

LISBETH OESTREICHER
AND OTHER PHOTOGRAPHERS
1902, Karlovy Vary (CZ) – 1989, Amersfoort (NL)
Bauhaus Album (Photo album with Bauhaus photographs from the collection of Lisbeth Oestreicher [1902–1989]), 1926–1930
Gelatin silver prints, various dimensions

Lisbeth Oestreicher became known for her weaving, woven designs, and work with textiles. She studied at the Bauhaus in Dessau from 1926 to 1930. This art school, founded in 1919 by architect Walter Gropius, existed for just fourteen years, yet it had an enormous impact all over the world. Its teaching program was based on a synthesis of the arts: the visual arts, architecture, and design were merged in both theory and practice. Like other modernist movements, the Bauhaus believed in the power of the new, in technology, and in the ability of art to create a better society. Foreign teachers like Wassily Kandinsky and László Moholy-Nagy gave the school international allure. With its exhibitions, festivities, unusually designed publications, photographs, and films, the Bauhaus was like a magnet to young artists and designers.
Lisbeth Oestreicher documented her time at the Bauhaus in great detail. She took photographs of herself, fellow students, teachers, lessons, and her surroundings. Her own photographs and those by other photographers were collected together in an album that has ended up in the Stedelijk collection, and is known as the *Bauhaus Album*. It gives a fabulous impression of life at the legendary art school.

Exhibition *Up to Now*, 2003

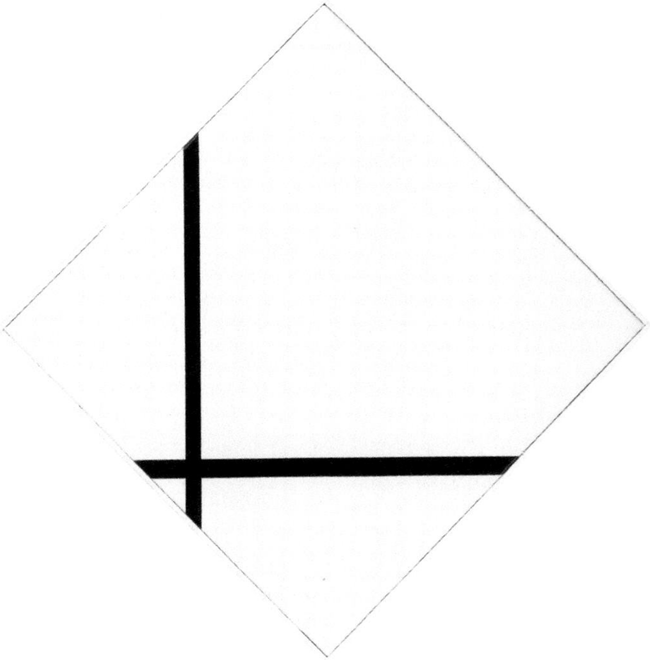

PIET MONDRIAN
1872, Amersfoort (NL) – 1944, New York, New York (US)
Ruitvormige compositie met twee lijnen (Lozenge Composition with Two Lines), 1931
Oil on canvas, 120.5 × 120 cm, acquired with the generous support of the Prins Bernhard Fonds, the Algemene Loterij Nederland and the Vereniging Rembrandt, 1988

Piet Mondrian was inspired by nature, by what he saw. His urge to create was accompanied by a desire to get as close as possible to the truth. Mondrian discovered that abstracting everything brought him closest to the "foundation of things." From 1914 onwards, he painted fewer and fewer recognizable representations of subjects like windmills, and an increasing number of "compositions" – paintings built up of lines, planes, and colors.

Mondrian sought a balance between form and color, and he believed that balance could be expressed only in a painting that possessed "universal calm." To achieve this, from 1917 he used only rectangular forms and the colors red, yellow and blue, or the "non-colors" white, gray, and black. Most of Mondrian's abstract paintings are rectangular or square, and are arranged around a central plane. In the early 1930s, however, he produced a series of lozenge-shaped paintings in black and white, with two intersecting lines as the ordering principle. In *Lozenge Composition with Two Lines* the intersection of the lines is so far off-center that it creates a tense opposition, while the lines and planes delicately balance each other. Together they constitute the harmony of universal relationships that Mondrian sought.

EVA BESNYÖ
1910, Budapest (HU) – 2003, Laren (NL)
Berlijn (Berlin), 1931–1932
Gelatin silver print, 50.4 × 47.9 cm, acquired with the generous support of the Ministry of Welfare, Health and Cultural Affairs, The Hague (NL), 1985

When Hungarian photographer Eva Besnyö arrived in Berlin in 1930, the city was the epicenter of new developments in film and photography. She encountered Russian film and the new photographic idiom of Alexander Rodchenko and László Moholy-Nagy, who were both experimenting with perspective. Rodchenko wrote, "The most interesting perspectives today are from the top down, from the bottom up and their diagonals."

Geometric lines and a high camera position became the defining characteristics of Besnyö's photographs. In *Berlin* she adheres strictly to this structure. This picture of a crossroads in Berlin shows a cyclist and a group of children. Thanks to the perspective and the moment, the shadows of the figures form geometric patterns. The photograph is a fine example of rigidly linear modernity, and is surprising partly for that reason; the quiet, empty streets in Besnyö's pictures belie the image of the bustling metropolis that was 1930s Berlin.

MARGUERITE WILDENHAIN-FRIEDLAENDER
1896, Lyon (FR) – 1985, Guerneville, California (US)
Five o'Clock, 1937
Manufactured by N.V. De Sphinx v/h Petrus Regout & Co., Maastricht (NL), glazed earthenware, various dimensions, gift of Franz Wildenhain, Putten (NL), 1940

French-Jewish artist Marguerite Friedlaender was one of the first students to enroll at the Bauhaus in Weimar, a progressive art academy which – like De Stijl – strove for a synthesis of design, art, and architecture, defined above all by simplicity, functionality, and craftsmanship, and all in the name of a higher cause: creating a better world. Friedlaender was also keen on a strong connection between the arts, crafts, and industry. She was already an influential ceramicist and teacher when, like many other socialist Bauhaus artists, she fled Nazi Germany in 1933. She and her husband, Franz Wildenhain, ended up in the small Dutch town of Putten, where they opened a pottery shop called 't Kruikje. The *Five o'Clock* tea set was designed during her time in the Netherlands, though in terms of its shape and execution – practical, functional, and devoid of ornamentation – it is pure Bauhaus. The clear forms are obviously derived from basic stereometric shapes. The milk jug, for example, is based on a cylinder, and the handles are conical. Friedlaender designed the modern-looking tea set in 1937 for the World Fair in Paris, where she won the Grand Prix. Unfortunately, it never went into production.
In 1940 Friedlaender left for the United States, where she founded her own pottery at the Pond Farm artists' colony in California and went on to inspire generations of ceramicists.

MAX BECKMANN
1884, Leipzig (DE) – 1950, New York, New York (US)
Doppelportrait von Quappi und mir (Double Portrait of the Artist and His Wife Quappi), 1941
Oil on canvas, 193.5 × 89 cm

Max Beckmann and his young wife, Mathilde von Kaulbach, fled Germany in 1937. The Nazis had labeled Beckmann's expressionist paintings, with their bright colors and heavy outlines, as *entartet* ("degenerate art"). On their way to America, the couple stopped in Amsterdam. When war broke out, what was meant to be a brief stopover turned into a ten-year stay. This was a highly productive period for Beckmann, during which he produced 280 paintings in his studio on Rokin. Nevertheless, only three Beckmanns are in public collections in the Netherlands. This double portrait is one of them. The faces are the most detailed feature of the painting, and have the greatest contrast of light and shade, with Beckmann using this device to emphasize the couple's mood. The painter looks despondent, wary. Quappi has placed her hand on his shoulder. Together, they have an aura of anxious resolve.

The portrait was painted between September 29, 1940, and February 8, 1941, a period of aerial bombings, chaos, and uncertainty. "I must not let anything unsettle me, please remember!" Beckmann noted in his journal. Is that why they are shown dressed for the outdoors, their legs already in motion, poised to go out?

KURT SCHWITTERS
1887, Hannover (DE) – 1948, Kendal (UK)
Ohne Titel (Um den Kern der Sache) (Untitled [Around the Core of the Matter]), 1941
Oil on linoleum, wooden ring, 104.5 × 91 cm, acquired with the generous support of the Mondriaan Fund and the Vereniging Rembrandt, 2004

Like other European artists, Kurt Schwitters sought to create new art from the ruins of the First World War. While Dadaists agitated for a destructive anti-art, Schwitters sought to make connections, preferably between everything in the world. He rekindled his creativity in an explosion of collages, poetry, music, pamphlets, and meetings at which he publicized (sang) his utopian ideas about art. In 1924 he found a name that connected everything he did and made: MERZ! Typical Merz artworks are assemblages made of all kinds of things: packaging, playing cards, fragments of posters, scraps of newspaper, paint, pencil.
This piece from 1941 shows how Schwitters later came to prefer abstract forms and primary colors, like his friends Theo van Doesburg and Hans Arp. Schwitters painted it while in a British internment camp, where he had been imprisoned as an "enemy alien" after fleeing Germany and then being exiled from Norway. The *objet trouvé,* the curtain ring to the left of center, recalls the familiar assemblages of Schwitters's earlier career.

CHARLEY TOOROP
1891, Katwijk aan Zee – 1955, Bergen (NL)
Arbeidersvrouw (Working-Class Woman), 1943
Oil on canvas, 150 × 119 cm

Charley Toorop was born into an artistic environment. The daughter of the famous symbolist painter, Jan Toorop, she met artists like Piet Mondrian (p. 51) while on holiday in Domburg, the Netherlands. She was a key figure in Dutch artistic circles, and had connections to the international avant-garde. Her house, "De Vlerken," in Bergen was an important meeting place for artists, poets, writers, and musicians in the 1930s. Despite her great affinity for the work of Mondrian and Bart van der Leck, Toorop developed her own highly realistic style, seeking to depict "animated reality" in her still lifes and portraits. She would paint life-sized, head-on portraits of laborers and farmers, relatives and friends, using angular forms and lines, strong light, and dark contrasts. In her desire to capture the essence of her subjects, Toorop also painted dozens of self-portraits, which trace her development as an individual and as an artist.

Working-Class Woman is one of Toorop's darkest paintings. Only the woman's skin and the wall to the right have any hint of color. The rest is black and white, like in a photograph or film. Many of Toorop's models look directly at the viewer, but the woman in the black dress does not seek contact with us. Her thoughts are elsewhere.

WILLEM SANDBERG
1897, Amersfoort – 1984, Amsterdam (NL)
Experimenta typografica 1, Lectura sub aqua, 1943
Manuscript, 21 × 25.3 cm

Willem Sandberg was director of the Stedelijk Museum from 1945 until 1962, but was also a prolific graphic designer. He believed museums were for everyone, for every day; "centers of life" rather than elite institutions. His acquisition and exhibition policy turned the Stedelijk into one of the world's leading modern art museums, with its own unique and very personal house style. Sandberg not only managed the museum, he also designed all its printed material. He felt its posters and catalogues should be "normal and vibrant." His graphic work appears simple and spontaneous, but this is largely due to the materials he chose. Sandberg often used simple brown card, but he is perhaps best known for his torn letters. He adopted this technique in an attempt to liberate himself from classical drawing. He liked the rough contours because, as in sculpture, the result was achieved by removing rather than adding something.

Sandberg's design method is magnificently displayed in *Experimenta typografica* – a set of booklets, design experiments that were carefully written, drawn, and pasted in the form of collages – that he produced while in hiding during the Second World War. Sandberg was a member of the artists' resistance, and one of the few to escape execution by the Nazis after an arson attack on the Amsterdam Public Records Office in 1943.

EMMY ANDRIESSE
1914, The Hague – 1953, Amsterdam (NL)
Amsterdam (Boy with Cooking Pan, Hunger Winter Amsterdam), 1944–1945
Gelatin silver print, 23.3 × 17.5 cm, gift from Bert Bakker (Uitgeverij Contact), Amsterdam (NL), 1976

Amsterdam, 1945. The final winter of the war. Cold, hunger, misery. This boy is on his way to the soup kitchen for something to eat. He is not the only one, but Emmy Andriesse deliberately omitted the others waiting in line. We see only this little fellow, with his serious face and his thin, bare legs. The picture gives us the chills. At the center of the image, his thin hand clutches the handle of the pan like a bird's claw, in a gesture that seems to encapsulate all the deprivations of the Hunger Winter, the Dutch famine of 1944 to 1945. Andriesse was part of a resistance group called the Underground Camera, along with fellow photographers like Cas Oorthuys, Carel Blazer, and Ad Windig. At great personal risk and using poor equipment, they secretly photographed raids, the persecution of the Jews, and the resistance. Before and for a short time after the war, Andriesse produced magnificent, more technically perfect photographs of other children, well-known artists, fashion, and Van Gogh's Arles, but the portrait of the little boy with the pan would remain her best-known image. His became the face that symbolized the final year of the war.

Exhibition *Alexander Calder*, 1969

ALEXANDER CALDER
1898, Philadelphia, Pennsylvania – 1976, New York, New York (US)
Suspended Composition of Small Leaves (Four Red Spots), ca. 1947
Painted aluminum and steel wire, 137 × Ø 135 cm

After studying mechanical engineering, Alexander Calder traveled from the United States to Paris in 1926. There he caused a sensation with his whimsical *Le Cirque Calder*, a miniature circus of steel wire, cork, fabric, and other materials, which he brought to life during performances. His first "mobiles" – a term coined by Marcel Duchamp – date from the early 1930s. In 1930 Calder visited Piet Mondrian and was deeply impressed by the movable colored rectangles the painter used to make compositions on the walls of his studio. Calder imagined how it would be if the rectangles were to be set in motion. His first spatial compositions in black, with red, yellow, and blue highlights, were therefore not inspired by three-dimensional sculpture, but by painting. Calder's wire structures attached to the ceiling seem light as a feather, and appear to float.
A breath of wind is enough to set the shapes moving. Although he also produced lithographs, jewelry, outdoor sculptures, and paintings, his mobiles have ensured that Calder has gone down in history as one of the founders of kinetic art.

J. Dubuffet 47

JEAN DUBUFFET
1901, Le Havre – 1985, Paris (FR)
Personnage hilare (Portrait de Francis Ponge)
(Hilarious Figure [Portrait of Francis Ponge]), 1947
Oil and plaster on cardboard, on canvas stretcher, 60.5 × 45.5 cm, gift of the artist, 1966

What is beauty? Jean Dubuffet had his own ideas about beauty and art, and they were quite at odds with conventional tastes. He believed children, the mentally ill, and other social outcasts were the makers of true art, an art that was instinctive, passionate, violent, and genuine. In other words, not "contaminated" by civilization. He called it *art brut*, and amassed a large collection of it.
This portrait of French poet and essayist Francis Ponge resembles a child's drawing in many ways. Dubuffet used plaster rather than paint for the round head that balances in quite a sinister way on the thin neck. He drew the broad grin using his finger. Dubuffet often used unusual materials in these primitive portraits, including asphalt, cement, glass, and sand. He chose different materials for each new series of works. He would experiment with paint in one, while in another he would use tree bark, banana peels, or butterfly wings. His search for raw expression eventually led to the creation of huge outdoor sculptures such as *Jardin d'email* (1973), located in the sculpture park at the Kröller-Müller Museum, in Otterlo (NL).

Collection presentation, 2012

KAREL APPEL
1921, Amsterdam (NL) – 2006, Zürich (CH)
Vragende kinderen (Questioning Children), 1949
Paint on wood, 105 × 67 × 17.5 cm

While Karel Appel was traveling by train through Germany shortly after the Second World War, he saw children begging for money and food at railway stations. This experience prompted his *Questioning Children* series, which he produced in 1948 and 1949. The painted relief is made of discarded wood. Appel nailed wooden blocks to a background made of planks and drew faces on them using dots and lines. The work brings together the children's will to survive and the artist's urge to create.

As one of the founders of the Cobra movement, Appel believed that authenticity and spontaneity were more important than aesthetic beauty. The Cobra artists wanted to produce art in complete freedom, and entirely rejected the views of the traditional art academies. Strongly influenced by Pablo Picasso (p. 91), Henri Matisse (p. 85), and Jean Dubuffet (p. 71), they strove to achieve a primary form of expression like that seen in children's drawings. In Appel's work this is reflected in the bright colors, simple shapes, and rough materials that evoke intuitive associations.

The power of these associations became apparent when Appel turned *Questioning Children* into a mural for the canteen of Amsterdam's City Hall. The staff protested, not wanting to be confronted with such misery while eating lunch. The children's huge eyes disappeared behind a wall and were not revealed again until 1959.

ED VAN DER ELSKEN
1925, Amsterdam – 1990, Edam (NL)
Vali Myers, Paris, 1951 (from: *Love on the Left Bank*, 1956)
Gelatin silver print, 23 × 18 cm

The life of photographer, filmmaker, and globetrotter Ed van der Elsken was closely interwoven with his work. This untitled photo comes from his first book, *Love on the Left Bank*, a photonovel that tells the fictional story of a group of young bohemians in postwar Paris. His intense images signified a break with the respectful but slightly distant documentary photography of a previous generation of Dutch photographers. Van der Elsken was not an observer, he was a partaker. His world, printed in velvety black and white, was that of the night, of drinking and smoking cannabis and dancing with wild abandon to jazz, of boys and girls living and loving on the street and in cheap hotels. This visual account of a passionate nihilism shows a completely different side of the "conservative" 1950s.
After leaving Paris, Van der Elsken returned to Amsterdam and, from 1971, lived in the countryside near Edam, which became his home base as he traveled the world, including several trips to his favorite destination, Japan. In his later work Van der Elsken increasingly played the role of art director, challenging his models to reveal themselves to his camera, entirely in accordance with the motto of his final, autobiographical film, *Bye*: "Show who you are."

Collection presentation, 1984

BARNETT NEWMAN
1905–1970 New York, New York (US)
Cathedra, 1951
Oil and acrylic on canvas, 243 × 543 cm, acquired with the generous support of the Vereniging Rembrandt, Theo van Gogh Stichting and NN, 1975

Barnett Newman tried to give the viewer an overwhelming emotional and physical experience that would make one aware of oneself and one's place in the universe. He worked on huge canvases, painting with intense, overpowering colors. He encouraged the visitors of his 1951 exhibition at the New York gallery of Betty Parsons to look at his paintings from close up, rather than from a distance. *Cathedra* was created that same year. Many of Newman's titles refer to the Bible or Jewish mysticism. *Cathedra* means "seat" or "throne," and for Newman it was linked to the vision of the biblical prophet Isaiah (Isaiah 6:1), in which he saw God sitting on a throne in the temple. Newman wanted to evoke the same exalting experience with this painting.

The intense, dark-blue field of color appears to be moving through the black haze of paint. This sea of heavenly blue is intersected in two places. The stripe in the center is sharp, clear, and white. The light-blue stripe to the right is thin and diffuse. Newman called these vertical bands "zips" and used them in almost all his work. Art historians have interpreted them as shafts of light, or as Giacometti-esque elongated human forms, but their formal function is clear: zips give us some visual purchase as we experience Newman's overwhelming paintings.

Exhibition *The Oasis of Matisse*, 2015

HENRI MATISSE
1869, Le Cateau-Cambrésis – 1954, Nice (FR)
La perruche et la sirène (The Parakeet and the Mermaid), 1952–1953
Gouache on paper, cut and pasted on paper mounted on canvas, 337 × 768.5 cm, acquired with the generous support of the Vereniging Rembrandt and the Prins Bernhard Cultuurfonds, 1967, restored with the generous support of the participants of the BankGiro Loterij

Henri Matisse painted in various styles over the course of his long career, but always with the same aim: "the essential thing is to spring forth." He was driven by a desire for balance, purity, and serenity. When he became confined to a wheelchair after surgery and could no longer paint, he began to cut shapes from painted sheets of paper. With the aid of assistants, he would stick them on the wall of his apartment in Nice, then shift and arrange them until he arrived at a composition that blended the foreground and background, forms and surrounding space, into a unified whole.

La perruche et la sirène is one of Matisse's last, and largest, *papiers découpés*. The colorful image features pomegranates, leaves, and – in a more central position – a parakeet and a mermaid, uniting the world above and below the water in a single composition. The many pinholes in the paper bear witness to the fact that the cut-outs were moved numerous times before they arrived at their final position in the composition. Though this is a flat image, the playful composition, abundant forms, and nuances of color draw the viewer into an overwhelming sea of images. Matisse regarded this spatial effect as vital. He described *La perruche et la sirène* as "a little garden all around me where I can walk."

Collection presentation, 2016

LUCIO FONTANA
1899, Rosario de Santa Fé (AR) – 1968, Comabbio (IT)
Concetto spaziale (Spatial Concept), 1953
Paint and glass on canvas, 76 × 57 cm, gift of Mrs. T. Fontana, Milan (IT), 1970

Lucio Fontana became world famous for his perforated canvases. Sometimes he would make a series of slightly curved cuts or small punctures in geometric patterns. At other times he would slash the canvas in a single gesture. The perforations are not lines as in a drawing, but openings into the space around the artwork. "When I work as a painter on my perforated canvases, I don't set out to make a painting," he once explained, "I want to open space, create new dimensions for art and allow them to be absorbed into the cosmos extending endlessly beyond the confines of the painting." He gave many of these works the title *Concetto spaziale*. In the manifestoes in which he explained his theories, Fontana referred to "new dimensions" and "the cosmos," but his art is in fact remarkably tangible, possibly because he was originally a sculptor who only turned to painting in his fifties. In *Concetto spaziale* the canvas is rough, the paint stiff, the holes jagged: the material has a very strong presence. The sparkling pieces of red glass enhance the materiality. At the same time they give the painting a festive feel, for however "damaging" Fontana's actions were, he performed them with a sense of elegance and style.

PABLO PICASSO
1881, Málaga (ES) – 1973, Mougins (FR)
Femme nue devant le jardin (Nude in Front of a Garden), 1956
Alkyd on canvas, 130.5 × 163 cm, acquired with the generous support of the Rembrandt Society, the Theo van Gogh Foundation and NN, 1981

In this 1956 painting a naked woman lies before open louver doors leading to a balcony that overlooks a garden in full bloom. It is an homage to Henri Matisse, whose many recumbent female nudes (Odalisques) were admired by Pablo Picasso and his fellow modernists. After Matisse's death in 1954, Picasso felt it was his duty to do something with the subject championed by his deceased friend. He said, "When Matisse died, he left me his Odalisques as a legacy." *Femme nue devant le jardin* is Picasso's interpretation of Matisse's notorious *Nu bleu* of 1907, in which a naked woman in shades of blue is seen against a background of plants. Picasso's roughly executed, angular interpretation is reminiscent of cubism, a style he had developed with a number of his contemporaries more than forty years previously. Cubist painters showed their subject from several perspectives at once. Here, too, the belly, breasts, buttocks, and facial features are shown from both the front and the side. Picasso also used the classic Odalisque subject to play with the tension between what can be seen and what is shown.

CONSTANT
1920, Amsterdam – 2005, Utrecht (NL)
Spatiovore, 1958–1959
Perspex, iron, aluminum, wood, 25 × 56 × 41 cm

One of the founders of the experimental Cobra group, Constant painted in an expressive and associative style. He believed that creativity would lead to freedom, and that spontaneity was of the utmost importance.
In the early 1950s Constant shifted his focus to designing three-dimensional environments. Along with architect Aldo van Eyck, he published texts on the integration of color and form in architecture. During this period Constant also started building architectural models, like *Spatiovore.* This and other structures eventually led to a grand design for a utopian city, New Babylon – a city in which all work would be automated and the residents would be free to spend their time relaxing and at play. Since everyone would be free to express their creativity, art as a profession would become obsolete.
Spatiovore illustrates Constant's idea of New Babylon, with living spaces suspended above the ground, where all the work would take place. Recreational areas could be reconfigured at will: the color, atmosphere, and size of each space would be adaptable. Constant regarded his models merely as suggestions. After all, it would be up to free human beings to shape their world according to their needs.

Collection presentation, 2016

YVES KLEIN
1928, Nice – 1962, Paris (FR)
L'accord bleu (RE 10), 1960
Paint, sponges and small stones on wood, 199 × 163 cm

Yves Klein did things no other artist had ever done. He patented a color, for example, which he called International Klein Blue. He also used models as brushes, and fire as a medium. *L'accord bleu (RE 10)* comes from the same year in which Klein signed the nouveau réalisme manifesto, which accorded reality itself the status of theme and medium. Klein focused on the non-material sides of reality. His desire to cross boundaries is reflected in the rounded corners, where the pigment runs into the surrounding space. The sponges and pebbles attached to the canvas evoke an extraterrestrial landscape. Klein hoped that the viewer would be transported into blue distances and return, full of visual intoxication, as a different person.
The work of "Yves le Monochrome," a nickname that refers to Klein's paintings in only one color, is the link between modernism and postmodernism. His desire to give the viewer a metaphysical experience is reminiscent of Mondrian and Malevich (pp. 51 and 35), while the creation of his public persona anticipated the methods of Andy Warhol (p. 117) and Joseph Beuys.

Gismo in the exhibition *Jean Tinguely Machine Spectacle*, 2016

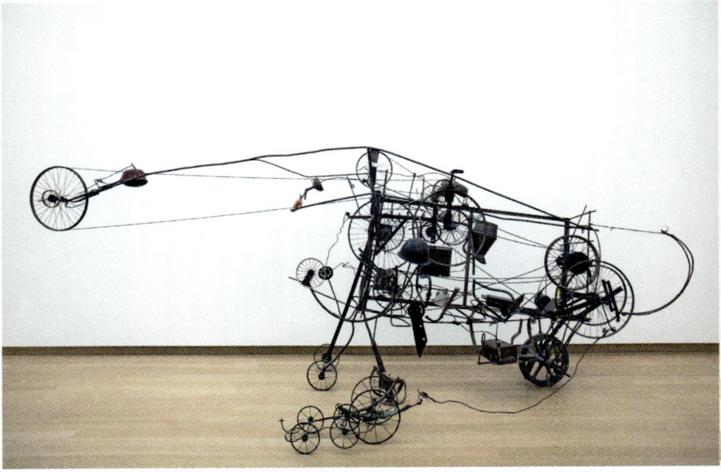

JEAN TINGUELY
1925, Fribourg – 1991, Bern (CH)
Gismo, 1960
Scrap metal, rubber, plastic, wood, electric motor, ca. 200 × 560 × 170 cm

"Everything moves. Immobility does not exist. Resist the anxious wish to fix the instantaneous," was Jean Tinguely's motto. He resisted the rules of art, the silent white spaces in which visitors pondered static paintings. In the 1950s and '60s, along with his contemporaries, Yves Klein and Daniel Spoerri (pp. 97 and 143), he attempted to break down the barrier between art and everyday life. He did so, among other things, by using objects he had found.
Gismo consists of wheels from bicycles, wheelbarrows, and toy baby carriages – all found in the scrap heap. Tinguely produced this piece shortly after returning from the United States, where he had learned to use electric welding equipment. He took *Gismo* and four other large machines from the same period on a spectacular parade through the streets of Paris, from his studio to a gallery. *Le Transport*, as this event would later become known, was a veritable happening, complete with flags and a band, full of chaos and joy and a bit of commotion, exactly as Tinguely liked it. After 1965, Tinguely and his life partner, Niki de Saint Phalle, made many pieces for public spaces, including the kinetic *Stravinsky Fountain* outside Centre Georges Pompidou in Paris.

BERND AND HILLA BECHER
Bernd: 1931, Siegen – 2007, Rostock (DE)
Hilla: 1934, Potsdam – 2015, Düsseldorf (DE)
Hochofen, Siegen, Westfalen (Blast Furnace, Siegen, Westfalen), 1961
Gelatin silver print, 40.3 × 30.3 cm, gift of Rudi Fuchs, 2001

Bernd and Hilla Becher always photographed the same things – water towers, grain silos, coal mines, gas tanks, and lime kilns – while documenting the changes in the industrial landscapes of Europe and America after the Second World War. Not only did they always choose the same subjects, they also never changed the way they photographed them: frontally, evenly lit (they preferred to work when it was cloudy), from the same distance and height, filling the frame, sharply focused, and in black and white. Because nothing is happening in the background, all attention is directed at the structure. The Bechers compiled series, or typologies, from the pictures in their archive. They would show twenty-four photographs of water towers in a regular grid, for example, neatly arranged as if they were rare flowers or butterflies.

From the 1970s onwards, their photographs became popular with conceptual artists, who preferred photography to the more "pretentious" art of painting. Minimalist artist Carl Andre (p. 159), who also worked with industrial materials like metal and brick, could relate to the way the Bechers categorized structures by function, form, and materials. Although the work of Bernd and Hilla Becher certainly has roots in the history of photography, their strict approach, working in series, was completely new and entirely dissimilar to any earlier form of the medium.

Collection presentation, 2016

LEE BONTECOU
1931, Providence, Rhode Island (US)
Untitled, 1961
Assemblage with metal frame, canvas and parchment, 136 × 188.5 × 37 cm

Until the 1960s, art by women was taken less seriously than that made by men, and was often simply dismissed as "feminine." The work of sculptor Lee Bontecou evaded this stereotype, and she has always been appreciated on her own merits. Her work has been exhibited alongside that of male "appropriation artists" like Jasper Johns and Robert Rauschenberg, who, like Bontecou, combined various materials (including found objects), media, and techniques (see "Scraps, Waste, Junk – Art," pp. 327–337).
Like much of Bontecou's work, *Untitled* is a combination of sculpture and painting. The bas-relief consists of a welded frame made of steel wire covered with pieces of leather and parts of canvas bags from the Laundromat beneath her studio in New York. Some of the fragments are painted; others have been blackened with a welding torch. Over the years Bontecou's work has been subject to various, wide-ranging interpretations. *Untitled* has also been interpreted in all kinds of ways, from sexual and violent to evidencing a fascination with nature. The artist herself has never specifically stated what her work means. However, she did say that it encompasses "as much of life as possible – no barriers – no boundaries – all freedom in every sense."

Exhibition *Schoonhoven*, 1973

JAN SCHOONHOVEN
1914–1994 Delft (NL)
R 61-3, 1961
Cardboard, newsprint, latex paint and wood, 114 × 70 cm

Jan Schoonhoven made art in his spare time. During the day he worked for the Dutch postal service, PTT, and in the evening, at his kitchen table, he produced the artworks for which he would become famous. Like Armando, Henk Peeters, and Jan Henderikse, Schoonhoven was seeking a more objective basis for art. Following the principles of the German Zero Gruppe, in 1960 he joined the Dutch Nul group. The name symbolized a new beginning, free of all the artistic ballast of the past. Spontaneity, emotionality, and subjectivity were all regarded as outmoded. From the early 1960s Schoonhoven began producing reliefs made of card on which he stuck newspaper, then reinforced them with triplex and painted them white using emulsion. To exclude personal preference and emotions as much as possible, he opted for the order and regularity of a grid. He chose the color white, as it gives the maximum light and shade effect. Schoonhoven used catalogue numbers as titles. *R 61-3* is the third relief he produced in 1961. He liked to emphasize the cool objectivity of his art and his deliberately "unartistic" approach. Yet the result is not cold. Today many people regard Schoonhoven's art as subtle and meditative.

DIANE ARBUS
1923–1971, New York, New York (US)
Child with a Toy Hand Grenade in Central Park, N.Y.C., photo 1962 / print Neil Selkirk 1971–1974
Gelatin silver print, 38.2 × 38.1 cm

Diane Arbus, one of the most widely recognized photographers of the twentieth century, created stirring black-and-white images that leave little room for indifference. Whether in her penetrating portrayal of people living on the fringes of society, or her sharp and occasionally merciless observations of celebrities, Arbus's focus is unwaveringly upon the subject. Arbus's famous photograph, *Child with a Toy Hand Grenade in Central Park, N.Y.C.*, was taken during an afternoon in New York in the early 1960s. It is the unique, unsettling quality so characteristic of her photographs that continues to provoke the controversy and allure that surrounds Arbus's work.

ELLSWORTH KELLY
1923, Newburgh, New York – 2015, Spencertown, New York (US)
Blue Red Rocker, 1963
Painted aluminum, 185 × 101 × 155 cm

The curves of a body, a bend in the road, or a flattened cardboard cup: Ellsworth Kelly drew inspiration from the visual qualities of everyday things. He thought that if you could turn off your mind and just look with your eyes, everything would become abstract. Kelly reduced motifs like a curve or a crease to tense, evenly painted areas of color divided by sharp contours. For this reason his work is known as "hard-edge painting." But, to Kelly, the expressive power of the fields of color were much more important than their boundaries. The freestanding – or, to use Kelly's words, "brought off the wall" – piece *Blue Red Rocker* is testament to the power of color. The red and blue of this folded ellipse have such an impact on each other that the piece seems to vibrate. It was Kelly's wish and intention that the viewer should experience this purely visual sculpture in an instinctive way. Color, composition, and surrounding space work together to conjure forth a physical experience. Anyone who accepts that this is a work without meaning is rewarded with an unparalleled sense of tranquility.

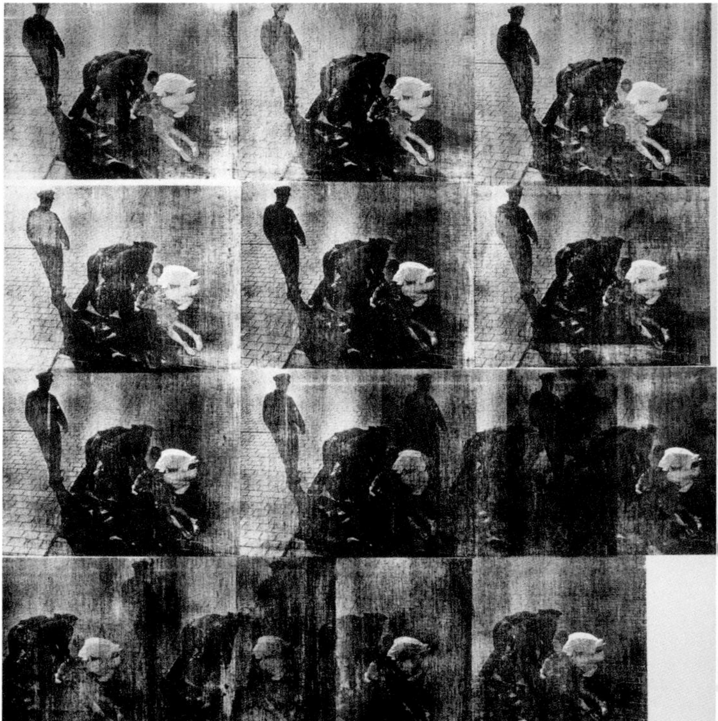

ANDY WARHOL
1928, Pittsburgh, Pennsylvania – 1987, New York, New York (US)
Bellevue II, 1963
Silkscreen ink and acrylic on canvas, 208.5 × 208.5 cm, acquired with the generous support of the Vereniging Rembrandt, 1978

The artists of the pop art movement drew inspiration from the consumerism and popular culture of the United States in the 1950s and '60s. They used advertising logos, packaging, and photographs of pop idols and film stars in their work, employing these things in a way that appeared playful, but was in fact often highly critical of society. Andy Warhol is the best-known of the pop artists, and also the most difficult to fathom. Warhol rarely made statements on what his work meant, and denied he had any social intentions. At the same time, his view that anything can be art prompted debate on the boundaries between life and art. Warhol made the everyday into art by painting, printing, photographing, filming, or making audio recordings.

Bellevue II is a police photograph reproduced thirteen times, with the raw, cropped edges of the images overlapping each other. The photo clearly shows that someone has just jumped out of the window at the Bellevue Hospital in Manhattan. Despite its morbid subject, the work has an aesthetic beauty similar to his screen prints of Marilyn Monroe or Campbell's soup cans. According to American art critic Robert Rosenblum, Warhol approached every subject with the same attitude: that of "aesthetic observer." He transformed a tragic suicide into art, just as he did with a Brillo box.

Willem de Kooning (left) and Stedelijk director Edy de Wilde
during the installation of the exhibition *Willem de Kooning*, 1968

de Kooning

WILLEM DE KOONING
1904, Rotterdam (NL) – 1997, East Hampton, New York (US)
Rosy-Fingered Dawn at Louse Point, 1963
Oil on canvas, 203.5 × 177.5 cm

Rotterdam-born Willem de Kooning became a figurehead of postwar American painting – abstract expressionism – with his swiftly rendered depictions of female figures. The woman, the landscape, and the merging of the two are recurrent themes in his work. *Rosy-Fingered Dawn at Louse Point* was named for one of De Kooning's favorite places on Long Island, where he would go by bike every day to look out over the water. He painted this abstract rendition of the idyllic landscape from memory at his studio in New York. The large expanses of color, pastel shades, and colors applied in successive layers of paint are typical of De Kooning. The pink is reminiscent of flesh, reminding us of his statement that "the landscape is in the Woman and there is Woman in the landscape." De Kooning's themes always remained the same, though he was constantly searching for new ways of converting sensual experiences into paint and, later, clay. De Kooning was the only abstract expressionist to produce sculptures. His bronze sculptures, based on small, hand-made forms, are related to his painting, depicting abstract human figures that merge with the ground. De Kooning donated thirteen sculptures to the Stedelijk Museum.

Collection presentation, 2012

YAYOI KUSAMA
1929, Matsumoto (JP)
Aggregation: One Thousand Boats Show, 1963
Assemblage, 60 × 130 × 265 cm, gift of the artist, 1965

Highly diverse and spanning over seven decades, the career of Japanese artist Yayoi Kusama cannot be characterized by a single practice or movement. At one point or another, Kusama has worked alongside the radical 1960s Nul group in the Netherlands, the corresponding German ZERO collective, the theater- and performance-based Japanese Gutai, and international Fluxus. Although her work demonstrates certain formal qualities similar to ZERO and the Dutch Nul group, such as repeating patterns and the use of white, it is also significantly different. Kusama was not concerned with achieving objectivity; her work is obsessive and sexually charged. *Aggregation: One Thousand Boats Show* was the first of Kusama's "Sex Obsession" pieces. The installation consists of a boat Kusama found on the street in New York while in the company of sculptor Donald Judd (p. 221), who had a studio in the same building, which she covered both inside and out with phallic shapes made from textile, along with two walls displaying 999 images of this same boat. Working with a limited budget at the start of her career, Kusama used a handheld sewing machine to create the phalluses, using old sheets and the stuffing of a discarded armchair. Having been raised in a highly conservative family, this work and the subsequently related *Infinity Rooms* represent the artist's confrontation of her fear of sex.

BAR

WIM T. SCHIPPERS
1942, Groningen (NL)
Signalement (Description), 1963
Video, black and white, sound, 29 min., 34 sec.

"Nothing is as enlightening as confusion," said Wim T. Schippers, who took great pleasure in disrupting the Dutch art and media world from the 1960s onwards. It began in 1961, when he and fellow student Ger van Elk (p. 185) published "The First (Provisional) A-dynamic Manifesto" in the weekly magazine *Vrij Nederland*. The young artists called for boring art, pathetic paintings, and "wonderfully gigantic and gigantically wonderful furniture." Schippers filled museum galleries with glass and salt, smeared the floor with peanut butter, and installed a giant turd sculpture in the garden of the VPRO broadcasting organization. Such amusing antics were typical of the liberal artistic climate of 1960s Amsterdam, (see "Counterculture," pp. 363–373) but Schippers has never stopped since. All his work as an artist and maker of radio and television programs is imbued with irony and absurdism. The one-off television broadcast from 1963, *Signalement*, is legendary. In this art program for broadcaster VARA, Schippers and Willem de Ridder "spotted" different trends in modern art. With ironic commentary and no further explanation, they introduced the "common man" to Arte Povera, ZERO, and Fluxus. Surrounded by a crowd of curious onlookers, Schippers emptied a bottle of cordial into the sea at Petten, the Netherlands. In this way, a program about art became art itself.

HANS HAACKE
1936, Cologne (DE)
Kondensationswürfel / Condensation Cube, 1963 / 1967 / 2010
Perspex, water, 76.2 × 76.2 × 76.2 cm

Photographs of processes, sculptures called *Systems*, installations about art influenced by context – everything in Hans Haacke's work is dynamic. Influenced by ZERO, an international group of artists who sought new materials with which to create art, in the early 1960s Haacke chose to use unstable materials like water and air in his work. *Condensation Cube* is one of his best-known pieces. The Perspex cube filled with water is a closed physical system in which the cycle of condensation constantly repeats itself. "The conditions are similar to those in a living organism that responds flexibly to its environment," Haacke once explained. "The picture of the condensation cannot be predicted with any accuracy. It changes at will, restricted only by statistical parameters. I like that freedom." Haacke began to focus on other types of systems towards the end of the 1960s, such as the political and sociological power structures surrounding art. His exploration of the ties between the art world, politics, and business inspired museum installations and works in public spaces. What Haacke intends to demonstrate is how an ostensibly autonomous work of art changes under the influence of its societal context, just as trapped moisture changes in response to temperature.

Collection presentation, 1970s

AS I OPENED FIRE, I KNEW WHY TEX HADN'T BUZZED ME...IF HE HAD...
BRAT!
THE ENEMY WOULD HAVE BEEN WARNED...
BRATATATATA!
THAT MY SHIP WAS BELOW THEM...

ROY LICHTENSTEIN
1923–1997, New York, New York (US)
As I Opened Fire, 1964
Acrylic (Magna) on canvas, 174.5 × 431 cm

In the early 1960s Roy Lichtenstein began using popular comic strips as the basis for his paintings. He admired the way comics could succinctly tell a complex story, and was fascinated by their graphic quality. He started using Ben-Day dots, the grid of dots used in cheap printed material for half-shades and additional colors. The magnified, hand-painted dots became the trademark of his work.

In *As I Opened Fire*, Lichtenstein used a fragment from the comic book series *All-American Men of War* containing fictional accounts of the experiences of American soldiers in the Second World War. Lichtenstein enlarged the original, but also altered the composition by zooming in on certain elements and omitting or abstracting others. Although a triptych is an ideal way to tell a story, Lichtenstein uses this series of images to emphasize the dynamic of repeating diagonals. Although he would later focus on other subjects, Lichtenstein's comic book paintings remain his best-known work.

FAGOTS-STAY

EDWARD KIENHOLZ
1927, Fairfield, Washington – 1994, Hope, Idaho (US)
The Beanery, 1965
Mixed media, ca. 253 × 670 × 190 cm

The Beanery is one of the best-known works by Edward Kienholz, and of the Stedelijk collection. Generations of visitors have strong recollections of their first encounter with his imitation bar. To enhance the pub atmosphere, Kienholz created an odor of mothballs, cigarette ash, beer, and urine that is pumped into the space using a fan. Constant background noise and jukebox music complete the experience.
Like Roy Lichtenstein (p. 133) and Andy Warhol (p. 117), Kienholz would reflect on city life in his work. However, he displays none of the detachment of the two pop artists. The everyday environments that Kienholz built using discarded objects highlight the destructive mechanisms behind modern life. "Children Kill Children in Vietnam Riots" is the headline on the newspaper by the entrance to *The Beanery*. This headline, from August 1964, was what prompted Kienholz to create this imitation of his local bar in Los Angeles. Apart from the landlord, everyone has a clock for a head, the hands fixed at ten minutes after ten for their eyebrows. Time is an important motif in *The Beanery*: the stopped clocks represent the time the patrons squander there without a thought for what is happening elsewhere in the world.

Collection presentation, 1970s

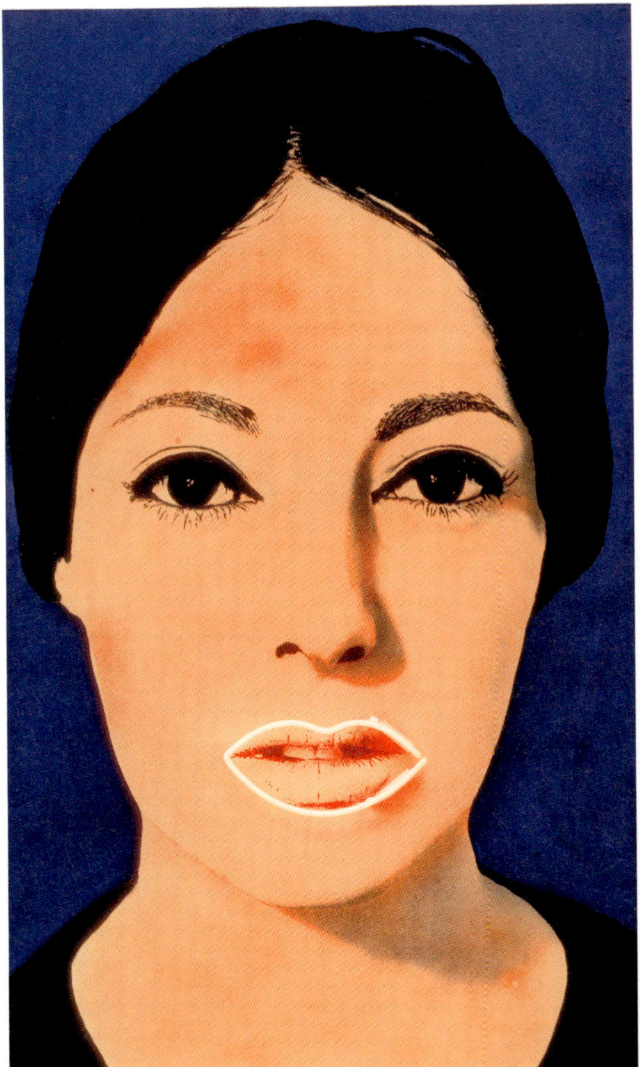

MARTIAL RAYSSE
1936, Golfe-Juan-Vallauris (FR)
Peinture à haute tension (High Voltage Painting), 1965
Cut-out photograph, ink, acrylic, fluorescent paint, flocking powder and neon light on canvas, 162.5 × 97.5 cm

Martial Raysse was one of the nouveaux réalistes. Like the American pop artists, this group of French artists focused on modern life. While most of them mainly used debris and discarded objects, Raysse in fact highlighted the pristine, artificial side of consumer society. The image of women in the mass media is a recurring theme in his work. His photographic works, for example, often feature mannequins wearing swimsuits, bathing caps, and sunglasses. Just as striking as these outfits is the fluorescent paint with which Raysse retouches his photographs. *Peinture à haute tension* also combines photography and painting. Like a second skin, orange paint covers the face of the anonymous woman with her made-up eyes and her slightly open mouth with its neon outline. Raysse also uses neon light, so bright that it drowns out the color of the paint. In this image the woman's face appears to be under high voltage. "Haute tension" can also be interpreted erotically. But this is no flesh-and-blood woman – the high voltage and her stereotypical beauty make her unattainable.

Exhibition *Daniel Spoerri*, 1971

DANIEL SPOERRI
1930, Galati (RO)
Table from the City Galerie Restaurant (from the series: *Restaurants*)
Mixed media, 120 × 120 × 40 cm, 1965

Swiss artist Daniel Spoerri was a founding member of the nouveau réalistes, a group of young artists who drew inspiration from popular culture, for instance, by incorporating found objects or materials into collages and assemblages. On September 25, 1965, Spoerri organized the opening of the "restaurant de la City Galerie," in the City Galerie in Zürich, Switzerland. Guests were to bring their own plates and cutlery, and art critics served the meal. After the dinner, Spoerri fixed all that was left over to the table top, which was to be mounted on the wall, preserving the dinner as a work of art.
Spoerri, who originally trained as a dancer, turned to making art in after 1959, starting with these *tableaux-pièges* ("picture-traps"): slightly grubby "still lifes" consisting of an array of stray objects from everyday life, fixed in the moment in which Spoerri decided to transform them. "A *tranche de vie*," Spoerri would call them ("a slice of life"). While he would acknowledge the ugliness and sadness of these waste landscapes, for him the picture-traps were mostly about the desire to move, and thus the will to live. In this respect, Spoerri's work is closely tied to that of his fellow nouveau réalistes, Niki de Saint Phalle and Jean Tinguely (pp. 181 and 101).

WENDY RAMSHAW AND DAVID WATKINS
Ramshaw: 1939, Sunderland (UK)
Watkins: 1940, Wolverhampton (UK)
Sunspex for *Something Special Ltd*, 1966
Cardboard and foil, printed, laminated and cut, 6.5 × 13 × 0.3 cm

Paper underwent a true revolution in the 1960s and '70s. For a short period of time, paper dresses were all the rage and architects such as Frank Gehry were making cardboard furniture pieces. Among the pioneers in the creative applications of paper was British jewelry designer Wendy Ramshaw. Having originally studied illustration and fabric design, Ramshaw and her husband, David Watkins, opened "Something Special" in the 1960s, a unique business venture in the production of paper jewelry. In creating designer jewelry – historically considered "luxury items" – out of cheap materials, Ramshaw's products not only revolutionized the uses of paper, but also began to question the notion of "preciousness" as a prerequisite of jewelry-making. Their designs were sold at various fashion boutiques and departments stores throughout London, but also through mail order. The flat-packed objects could be assembled by the buyer after delivery. Ramshaw often illustrated her jewelry with the Day-Glo colors characteristic of 1960s fashion, making them highly attractive to the general British public. This pair of mock-sunglasses depicts a pair of oversized eyes in Ramshaw's characteristically colorful geometric style, embodying the fun-loving, relaxed atmosphere of the "Swinging Sixties" in Britain.

Exhibition *Perspectief op textiel* (*Perspective on Textile*), 1969

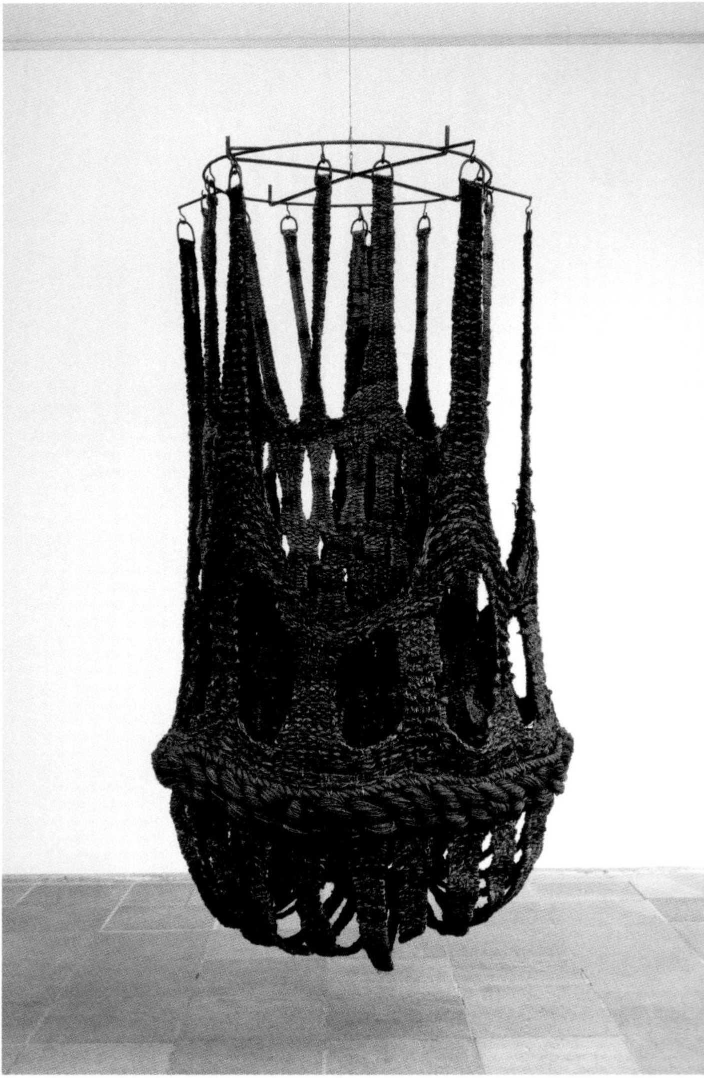

JAGODA BUIĆ
1930, Split (HR)
L'ange chassé (Fallen Angel), 1967
Woven and knotted sisal, 260 × Ø 145 cm

In 1967 Stedelijk director Edy de Wilde visited the São Paulo Art Biennial. Struck by the work of Croatian artist Jagoda Buić, De Wilde purchased her groundbreaking *Fallen Angel*, returning home to Amsterdam with the first-ever fiber sculpture to join the collection of the museum. Buić, who originally began as a costume and stage designer for the Croatian National Theater, had turned to a more artistically oriented practice in 1961, first with her hanging textiles and later with her fiber sculptures. *Fallen Angel*, in fact, was Buić's first hanging fiber sculpture, and signals a pioneering shift in the medium of textile.

Because hanging tapestries have traditionally been viewed as figurative and narrative images, they were always compared with painting, yet Buić's hanging sculpture comes loose from the wall and is the story, instead of referring to something outside itself. Its large size, industrial materials, and abstraction sooner bring to mind, for instance, the minimalist sculpture of Carl Andre or Donald Judd (pp. 159 and 221). *Fallen Angel* therefore makes short work of the gendered associations of weaving and crocheting. Buić, in other words, uses these "typically female" crafts to create monumental art. This makes *Fallen Angel* a revolutionary work of art .

new
alphabet

a
possibility
for
the
new
development

een
mogelijkheid
voor
de
nieuwe
ontwikkeling

une
possibilité
pour
le
développement
nouveau

eine
möglichkeit
für
die
neue
entwicklung

an
introduction
for
a
programmed
typography

WIM CROUWEL
1928, Groningen (NL)
New Alphabet, 1967
Steendrukkerij De Jong & Co, Hilversum (NL), lithograph, 25 × 25 cm

In 1963 Wim Crouwel co-founded Total Design, a design agency which would define trends with its functional, austere designs for over twenty years. Between 1963 and 1985, Crouwel shaped the identity of the Stedelijk Museum. His nickname, "System General," says it all: in order to standardize all of the museum's printed material, he introduced fixed formats, patterns, and even a new font, *Archetype Stedelijk*.
Crouwel was very interested in computers. He observed that graphic fonts had not evolved along with technology, and so in 1967 he designed *New Alphabet.* The highly simplified letters are made of horizontal and vertical lines, based on a rectangular grid of 5 x 9 pixels. Somewhat difficult to read, and without capitals, *New Alphabet* sparked fierce debate among designers. Crouwel's design philosophy also had its supporters and detractors. He believed that a design should inform rather than seduce. In his view the design profession was there to serve, and had a subordinate role. His outspoken views greatly influenced many designers, and continue to do so to this day.

Exhibition *The Temporary Stedelijk 2*, 2011

ESCALATED
FROM TIME TO TIME
OVERLOADED
FROM TIME TO TIME
REVOKED
HAVING FROM TIME TO TIME A RELATION TO

TAPIO WIRKKALA
1915, Hangö – 1985, Helsinki (FI)
Three vases from the *Bolle* series, 1967
Manufactured by, Venini & Co, Murano (IT), glass (*incalmo* technique),
h. 32, h. 25.8 and h. 46 cm

Finnish artist Tapio Wirkkala was a key figure in the regeneration of the applied arts in the Nordic countries after 1945. He was trained as a sculptor but from the 1950s onwards concentrated on designing industrial products. Wirkkala used all kinds of materials, from glass to wood, and from metal to plastics.
Wirkkala was inspired by craft traditions, and believed a designer must understand how products are made in practice. Another important source of inspiration for Wirkkala is the landscape and nature of Scandinavia. The forms of leaves, insects, birds, coconuts, and bones, as well as the turbulence of water and ice formations, recur in both his mass-produced and unique pieces.
In 1965 Wirkkala was commissioned by the Venetian glassworks company Venini. Traveling to Venice to work with the renowned glass blowers of Murano, Wirkkala intensely researched the history of Venetian glass and experimented with the incredibly difficult sixteenth-century *incalmo* technique, in which two or more glass elements are fused at high temperature. The 1967 *Bolle* series was the result of this collaboration. With his apt sensibility for his environment, Wirkkala translated the calm reflections of the Venetian lagoons and the soft colors of Titian and Tintoretto into a series of vases.

MARTHA ROSLER
1943, Brooklyn, New York (US)
Bowl of Fruit (from the series: *Body Beautiful, or Body Knows No Pain*), ca. 1965–1972
Photo montage, inkjet print, 50.8 × 40.6 cm

American artist Martha Rosler uses her work to expose various social problems. She made *House Beautiful: Bringing the War Home* between 1966 and 1972 as a strident protest against the Vietnam War. She cut out photographs of American soldiers and Vietnamese people who had been impacted by the war from *Life* magazine, then pasted them into pictures of comfortable, luxurious interiors from the magazine *House Beautiful*. This was her take on "the living room war," as the Vietnam War came to be known in the United States, referring to the fact that television brought shocking images of the conflict into people's living rooms. Rosler did not, incidentally, intend the montages solely as works of art, but as images for flyers that could be handed out during demonstrations. She added new images to the series in 2004 and 2008, in response to the Iraq War.

Besides criticizing political events, Rosler also often comments on power relationships between men and women, as seen in the video *Semiotics of the Kitchen*, a parody of cooking shows, or the series *Body Beautiful, or Beauty Knows No Pain*, in which she combines pictures from *House Beautiful* with naked women from *Playboy*.

CARL ANDRE
1935, Quincy, Massachusetts (US)
10 × 10 Altstadt Lead Square, 1967 / 1976
Lead plates, each 50 × 50 cm, in total 500 × 500 cm

Carl Andre is a poet and sculptor. He is not, however, a sculptor who hews shapes from stone or carves them from wood. Andre uses rough materials, like blocks of wood, bricks, or metal plates of the same size and shape, which he arranges in a simple geometric pattern. He adds nothing: no screws to attach the blocks, no raised plinth on which to display the sculpture. He always presents his work on the floor, installing each new piece himself. All the elements can therefore be moved by one person. Andre needs the act of shifting and maneuvering to enable him to think in tangible shapes. His choice of materials reveals his preference for the weighty and tactile. His work, he explains, is not an intervention in the material but an intervention in the space.
10 × 10 Altstadt Lead Square consists of a hundred lead plates that section off part of the museum floor. The neat 10 x 10 grid contrasts with the roughly cut, cumbersome material. Although the lead square subtly merges with the floor beneath it, visitors are nevertheless drawn to it, the adjacent plates inviting them to stand on and walk over them.

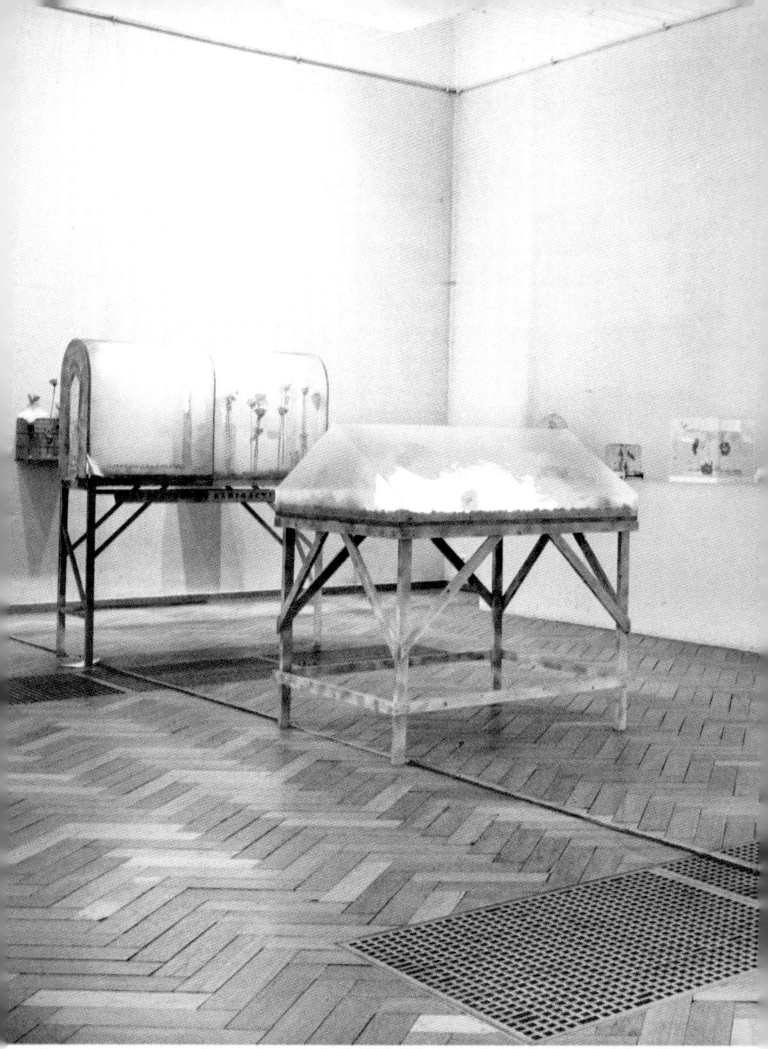

Exhibition *Tetsumi Kudo*, 1972

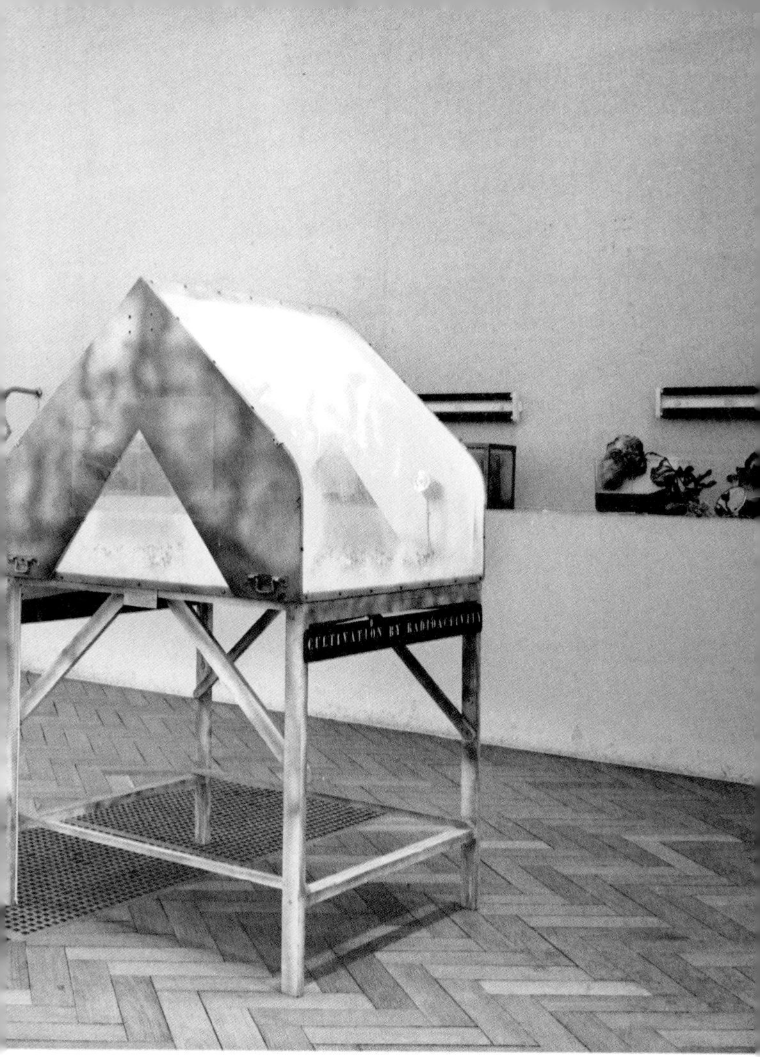
CULTIVATION BY RADIOACTIVITY

TETSUMI KUDO
1935, Osaka – 1990, Tokyo (JP)
Cultivation by Radioactivity in the Electronic Circuit, 1968
Mixed media, 80 × 98 × 100.5 cm, gift Ritsaert ten Cate, 1991

Following the destruction of Hiroshima and Nagasaki in 1945, the contemporary art scene in Japan underwent a major revolution. Artists were suddenly faced with painful memories of the past and yet hope for the future, thrusting artistic practice into suspension between reflection and experimentation. A major figure of the "anti-art" movement emerging in Tokyo in the late 1950s was Tetsumi Kudo.
The sculpture *Cultivation by Radioactivity in the Electronic Circuit* appears almost like a miniature greenhouse. Yet Kudo manipulates this positive association by painting the work a sickly lime green, inserting an artificial neon light in the cramped space, and implanting moss-like mesh lumps along the edges. The greenhouse, a place for light and natural growth, is transformed into a distinctly inauthentic, manufactured environment. Driven by a critique of the society in which he lived, Kudo's work was often dystopic in its reflection on the economically driven consumerism that emerged following the Second World War, as well as the way in which humans interacted with the environment in this dawn of a new age.

Exhibition *Revolution in the Air*, 2003

EMMY VAN LEERSUM
1930, Hilversum – 1984, Amersfoort (NL)
Driehoek (Triangle), *Vouw* (Fold), *Cirkel* (Circle), 1968
Bracelets, stainless steel, 3.5 × Ø 7.8 cm / 5 × Ø 7.5 cm / 5 × Ø 7.8 cm

The opening of the 1967 exhibition *Edelsmeden 3*, featuring the work of design duo Gijs Bakker and Emmy van Leersum, is one of the most memorable evenings in the history of the Stedelijk. Against a backdrop of electronic music and flashing lights, three models showed dresses designed by the duo, complete with matching jewelry, the most notorious of which were huge aluminum necklaces. Amsterdam fashion lovers went wild, but the press did not understand why the two did not make decorative jewelry. Their answer, "A woman is not a Christmas tree," caused some dismay. Van Leersum was not interested in the conservative world of jewelry. She even found the word itself prissy and unnecessary. "Wearable objects" was what she called her experimental geometric forms made of non-precious metals like stainless steel and aluminum. This was entirely in line with Van Leersum's views: forthright and unconventional. Her work was popular with a young generation of women whose every word and action, everything they wore, was testament to their liberation. These three bracelets are not therefore intended as ornament or status symbol, but as a way of expressing the personality of the wearer.

BRUCE NAUMAN
1941, Fort Wayne, Indiana (US)
My Name as Though It Were Written on the Surface of the Moon, 1968
Neon, 30 × 549 × 7 cm

For this artwork, American artist Bruce Nauman had his own name written in neon. Each letter is used six times. The preliminary studies for the piece consist of pictures of the letters on sheets of paper, which Nauman stuck together and then photographed from different distances. This gives the name a slightly convex appearance, an effect mirrored in the neon version. Nauman made it in 1968, just after the first photographs of the surface of the moon appeared in the newspaper, and shortly before the first moon landing.
Writing one's name is an act of appropriation. In the context of art, signing something is even more laden with meaning, as a signature lends a work authenticity. By turning his name into a work of art, Nauman was in fact signing part of the space, immediately raising the question of what it is to be an artist in the modern age. His choice of neon was also related to this same question. Nauman was one of the first artists to work with this material, which had previously only been used in advertising.

CARL ANDRE
ROBERT BARRY
DOUGLAS HUEBLER
JOSEPH KOSUTH
SOL LEWITT
ROBERT MORRIS
LAWRENCE WEINER

First Edition
1000
December 1968

Siegelaub/Wendler. . . . . New York, N. Y.

SETH SIEGELAUB
1941, Bronx, New York (US) – 2013, Basel (CH)
Xerox Book, 1968
Artists' book, 28 × 21.4 cm

The *Xerox Book* is a group exhibition in the form of a book. It was conceived by gallery owner, publisher, researcher, archivist, collector, and bibliographer Seth Siegelaub. As an exhibition maker, he played a key role in the emergence of conceptual art in the late 1960s. For Siegelaub, the idea behind art was more important than its execution. Artists did not need a gallery or museum to show their work: a book, picture post-card, poster, or symposium was an equally good place to exhibit it. "My gallery is the world now," Siegelaub said.

The *Xerox Book* contains twenty-five-page contributions from seven artists on the idea of reproduction. At first, Siegelaub wanted to have everything photocopied, but the technique was still imperfect in the late 1960s, and also very expensive. When photocopier manufacturer Xerox Corporation rejected his request for sponsoring in kind, he opted for the more common and less expensive offset printing to produce one thousand copies. The contributions from Carl Andre, Robert Barry, Douglas Huebler, Joseph Kosuth, Sol LeWitt, Robert Morris, and Lawrence Weiner were first photocopied and then printed on standard US letter format.

NOUS SOMMES TOUS
INDÉSIRABLES

ATELIER POPULAIRE
1968, Paris (FR)
Nous sommes tous indésirables (We are all undesirables), 1968
Silkscreen print, 49 × 32 cm

In May 1968 Paris was a site of chaos. Following the outbreak of student protests in the city several months prior, demonstrations against the conservative government of Charles de Gaulle swept through France. Protesters were demonstrating against the high unemployment rate, the bureaucracy, and the low wages for workers. Doing their part in the protests, the students at the School of Fine Arts occupied their school's graphic workshop, dubbing it "Atelier Populaire" – the people's workshop. There they worked, anonymously and collectively, on the production of posters to further their cause. With their quickly drawn images and simple lettering, the posters are highly effective and express the most important ideas behind the protests. Centered around slogans, with expressive lettering and printed in a single color (which was faster to produce), these posters filled the streets of Paris.

One of the most famous posters stemming from the atelier is entitled *Nous sommes tous indésirables* (We are all undesirables), and depicts in black-and-white contrast a photo of the laughing face of charismatic student leader Daniel Cohn-Bendit as he faces the police. The poster expresses solidarity with Cohn-Bendit, who, as son of German-Jewish refugees, faced expulsion by De Gaulle as an "undesirable." In this poster, however, the image is closely cropped on Cohn-Bendit, rendering the officer he faces merely a dark mass.

Excitement: An Exhibition by Rudi Fuchs, 2016

JAN DIBBETS
1941, Weert (NL)
Perspective Correction – My Studio II, 1969
Photographic print on linen, 115.5 × 115.8 cm

In 1967 Jan Dibbets stopped painting and turned his attention to photography. At that time many conceptual artists used photographs to document their work, yet Dibbets regarded photographs not as a means, but an end. In his photographic works he alters visible reality, transforming it into abstract images full of visual ambiguities.
Dibbets's photographs betray his love of architecture. Windows are a recurring theme in his work, as is the relationship between viewer and space. *Perspective Correction – My Studio II* is also about the perception of space. The square seems to be in front of the image. But if you look closely, you see that it has been stuck on the floor and photographed in such a way that the perspective is no longer correct. This "perspective correction" robs the studio of its depth, turning it into a flat image.
In his series of panoramas of the Netherlands, Dibbets also alters the perspective such that the taut line of the horizon starts to move.
Dibbets is famous for his contribution to the 1969 exhibition *Op losse schroeven: situaties en cryptostructuren* (*Everything Is Uncertain: Situations and Cryptostructures*), for which he excavated the corners of the Stedelijk Museum to expose the foundations, placing the museum on a pedestal and causing it to "wobble" (p. 352).

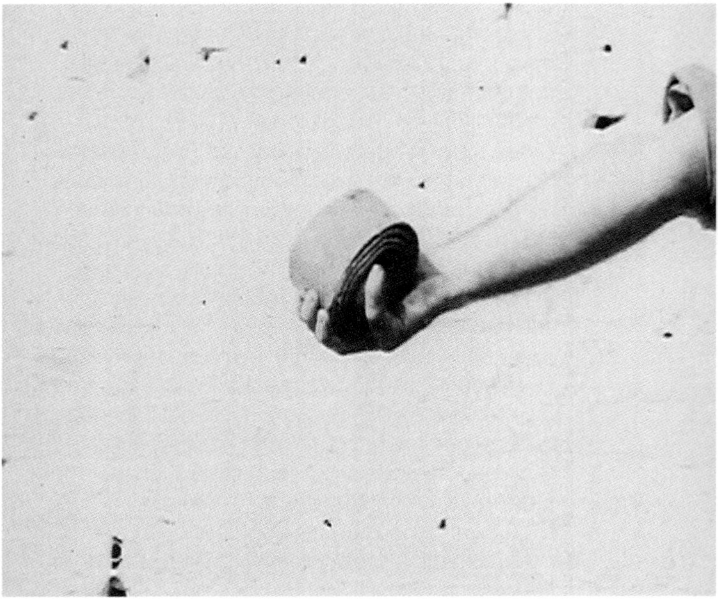

RICHARD SERRA
1939, San Francisco, California (US)
Hand Lead Fulcrum, 1969
Video, black and white, 2 min., 40 sec.

Though perhaps most well known for his monumental sculptural installations, American artist Richard Serra is also widely renowned for his experimental videos of the 1960s and '70s. Some of Serra's earliest videos include the *Hand and Process* series, a group of black-and-white videos depicting the artist's hands performing certain actions. Each video from the series was shot in one take and lasts three to four minutes. In his 1969 video *Hand Lead Fulcrum,* Serra's outstretched hand holds a lead cylinder. As the video continues, the artist's arm becomes increasingly tired and begins to shake. Having begun at the top of the screen, his arm slowly lowers under the weight of the object, and the video concludes with the disappearance of his hand at the bottom edge of the frame. Unlike traditional film, which is guided by a narrative structure, this work merely calls attention to the portrayed object in space, rather than a particular narrative. In this way, Serra's videos of this period were fundamental to the development of process-based art.

NIKI DE SAINT PHALLE
1930, Neuilly-sur-Seine (FR) – 2002, San Diego, California (US)
Tête blanche (White Head), 1970
Polyesther, acrylic, 230 × 223 × 97 cm

Since the early 1960s, Niki de Saint Phalle has maintained a remarkable presence in the Stedelijk Museum. A major participant in the highly popular 1962 exhibition *Dylaby* (short for "Dynamic Labyrinth"), De Saint Phalle was known for her daringness in experimentation as a member of the nouveaux réalistes group. As a playwright, sculptor, costume designer, creator of large-scale installations, filmmaker, painter, and theater set designer, De Saint Phalle left almost no medium unexplored. Her multimedia approach is epitomized in her 1966 installation at the Moderna Museet in Stockholm, entitled *Hon-en-Katedral*: a gargantuan sculpture of a reclining woman made in collaboration with Swiss artist Jean Tinguely. Via the vagina, visitors entered a circus-like interior fun house.
De Saint Phalle originally began to experiment with sculpture after meeting Tinguely (p. 101) in 1956 and agreeing to collaborate. Reflected in *Tête blanche*, her two-meter-tall, freestanding sculpture, are influences from De Saint Phalle's earlier "Nanas," of which *Hon* is a monumental example: robust female sculptures whose brightly colored, rounded forms have often been thought to highlight feminine power. In *Tête blanche* the large lips and plump eyes and nose depict a vigorously feminine figure, one whose overemphasized female qualities render her more goddess than woman.

CLAES OLDENBURG
1929, Stockholm (SE)
Saw (Hard Version II), 1971
Aluminum, wood, paint, 240 × 136 × 267 cm

Claes Oldenburg drew inspiration from everyday objects. Hamburgers, lipsticks, wash basins, and other perfectly ordinary items were transformed in his hands. "I'd like to get away from the notion of a work of art as something outside of experience, something that is located in museums, something that is terribly precious," he has said. His outsized sculptures brought humor into museums, and were also a salute to modern American culture.

Saw (Hard Version II) looks like a saw, but both the material and the scale have been changed. Oldenburg's version is huge, and the blade has three folds in it. These adaptations underline the fact that Oldenburg viewed the saw as a sculpture, and therefore also as an art object. The first time he offered his sculptures for sale (from December 1961 to January 1962), he did so in his own shop in New York's East Village, known as "The Store." Oldenburg made and sold sculptures there for prices ranging from twenty-five to five hundred dollars. The atmosphere in The Store was more like a local supermarket than a serious art gallery.

GER VAN ELK
1941–2014, Amsterdam (NL)
The Symmetry of Diplomacy I, 1971
Chromogenic color print, acrylic, two parts, each 62.5 × 62.5 cm

The codes and conventions in art and everyday life are a recurring theme in Ger van Elk's work. His photographs, slides, and films take a humorous look at all kinds of things we take for granted, like clichéd images and entrenched traditions. The series *The Symmetry of Diplomacy* was inspired by newspaper pictures of politicians officially welcoming foreign guests, in which the setting and the decor are perfectly symmetrical. Van Elk analyzes the staged imaged by retouching the photo with paint and inserting himself as a diplomat, or by moving people or dressing them in different clothes. Van Elk understood back in the early 1970s that photography can be used to manipulate. He turned the conventions of the medium upside down and used photography not to document reality, but to create an illusion. His photographic illusions raise questions about the "artist's obsession with creating a new reality." In a 1977 interview he said, "What I want is a realistic depiction of non-realistic situations."

GEORG BASELITZ
1938, Deutschbaselitz (DE)
Fingermalerei - Akt (Finger Painting - Nude), 1972
Oil on canvas, 200 × 163 cm

Georg Baselitz is the pseudonym of Hans-Georg Kern, taken from the name of the village where he was born in 1938, Deutschbaselitz, in what would later become the German Democratic Republic. He began painting his subjects upside down in 1969, and it pleased him so much he remained faithful to this method until the end of his career. The inversion gives the painting an abstract quality, and it allowed Baselitz to work from nature without the representation of the subject commanding all the attention. Or, as he himself explained, "An object painted upside down is suitable for painting because it is unsuitable as an object."
In this work the focus is on the act of painting. In German, *Fingermalerei* means "finger painting," and the word *Akt* has an appropriate double meaning: both an act or deed and a nude study. Baselitz did indeed apply the paint with his fingers, a technique he started using in 1972, describing it as "non-style." *Fingermalerei – Akt* may be a self-portrait, and it is one of a group of realistic nudes, all of which were painted in the same year.

PHILIP GUSTON
1913, Montreal (CA) – 1980, Woodstock, New York (US)
Painting, Smoking, Eating, 1973
Oil on canvas, 197 × 263 cm, acquired with the generous support of the Vereniging Rembrandt and Mrs. Guston, 1983

Philip Guston had already made a name for himself as an abstract expressionist painter when, in the late 1960s, he changed course entirely and began producing figurative art. While the German painter Georg Baselitz (p. 39) depicted his subjects upside down to emphasize that, for him, it was all about the painting, Guston came to the opposite conclusion: that painting derived its meaning from its potential to capture reality in an image. Upon further consideration, he found abstract painting to be ridiculous.

In *Painting, Smoking, Eating* we see the artist smoking while lying in bed with a plate of poutine (a popular Canadian dish from Quebec made with French fries covered with cheese curds and gravy) on his chest. The gray-pink palette creates an uncomfortable atmosphere. The one-eyed head in the shape of a lima bean is also disturbing. The misshapen head and pile of shoes are recurring motifs in Guston's work, which also often features Ku Klux Klan supporters, nooses, cigarettes, and clocks.

At the time when Guston painted *Painting, Smoking, Eating* his excessive lifestyle was already impacting his health. The grotesque works from this period clearly illustrate his obsession with death, but the sensual effect of the paint softens the morbid subject matter.

.OES VAN DER HORST
919, Noordwijk – 2012, Amsterdam (NL)
Vie heeft er in mijn bed geslapen? (Who's Been Sleeping in My Bed?), 1974
Hand braided polyethylene, aluminum, 191 × 132.5 cm

In the fairy tale of Snow White, the seven dwarfs return home one day to find their house in in disarray. "Who has been drinking from my mug?" they ask, and "Who has been sleeping in my bed?," only to discover the sleeping Snow White. Loes van der Horst poses the same question in the title of this hanging textile work – a phrase which seems to simultaneously accuse and invoke the help of the viewer. Gently drooping in the center, the work also seems to suggest the recent departure of an anonymous sleeper.

Van der Horst's textile work often suggests a broader social message regarding the role of women in the arts. As textile-making was traditionally associated with "women's work," in comparison to the "masculinity" associated with painting, Van der Horst here subverts this reference by creating a white, rectangular, hanging textile – suspiciously similar qualities to those of a painter's canvas.

Van der Horst's manipulation of the surface of the painting also situates itself within the art historical canon by referring to artists of the ZERO movement, such as Jan Schoonhoven and Lucio Fontana, who used white paintings as the site of surface experimentations, such as the slicing open of a blank canvas. While Schoonhoven gave the white surface relief and Fontana carved it with a knife, Van der Horst took command of the surface by creasing or rumpling it, thereby making the experiments of her male ZERO colleagues her own.

Exhibition *Holy Inspiration: Religion and Spirituality in Modern Art* at the Nieuwe Kerk in Amsterdam, 2008

Wereldcultuur bestaat, maar is geen afgerond geheel. Er is
Francesco Clemente, 1981
There is a world culture, but it's not something full. There is an emptiness in
Francesco Clemente, 1981

NAM JUNE PAIK
1932, Seoul (KR) – 2006, Miami, Florida (US)
TV Buddha, 1974
Video installation, closed-circuit, eighteenth-century Buddha statue, 160 × 215 × 80 cm

In the 1960s television developed into the ideal mass medium. Nam June Paik was one of the first artists to explore the artistic potential of the new medium. He did this in a highly versatile and unorthodox way. Paik, who emerged from the Fluxus movement, can equally be seen as a musician, visual artist, inventor, or philosopher. Paik used image manipulation in his installations to expose the mechanism behind television, overwhelming the viewer with a deluge of images. Nonetheless, *TV Buddha* is remarkably meditative. The antique Buddha statue seen on the screen of the small television is filmed on the spot by a video camera, making it appear as if the Buddha is watching himself. Thus, past and present, Eastern enlightenment and Western technology, sit in eternal mutual contemplation. The meditation is disturbed only by museum visitors walking in and out of the video image. While Paik explores the true nature and introspective power of television as a medium in *TV Buddha*, in other work he principally questions the position of the viewer. Are we condemned to watch passively, or can we also play an active role?

SIMONE FORTI
1935, Florence (IT)
Angel, 1975–1977
Holographic print, incandescent light bulb, plastic, wood, 151 × 41.2 × 40.7 cm

Artist, dancer, choreographer, and writer Simone Forti was born in Italy but moved to the United States at the age of four. In the late 1950s, as a young dancer, she joined the experimental art scene in New York, where artists sought to break down the barriers between makers and audience in their happenings and performances. Her *Dance Constructions* were first performed in 1960. The performances were based on simple movements and involved everyday objects, like balancing on a seesaw, hanging on a rope, or embracing someone. Forti gave the dancers a number of rules, but otherwise they were free to improvise.

Forti began studying the movements of animals in the late 1960s. *Angel* is about the relationship between breathing and flying. Forti used an entirely new technique in this work: the hologram. To make the hologram, she used separate film frames of herself making a flying movement on a revolving platform. Thanks to a slight delay in the technique, her left arm moves first, then her right. The viewer walks around the work to set the hologram in motion, thus becoming part of the choreography.

MARINA ABRAMOVIĆ AND ULAY
Abramović: 1946, Belgrade (RS)
Ulay: 1943, Solingen (DE)
Breathing Out / Breathing In (performance 10), 1977
video, color, sound, 17 min., 5 sec.

Marina Abramović and Ulay were an artistic unit for twelve years. The contrast between male and female, and also the melding of the two, was a recurring theme in their performances. In the 1980s the performances were inspired by rituals, but in the 1970s they often resembled a physical or mental struggle that sometimes drove the two artists to extremes.
In *Breathing Out/Breathing In*, which was performed at the Stedelijk Museum in 1977, Abramović and Ulay went so far that they began to shake, and almost lost consciousness. The performance began with Ulay taking a deep breath of oxygen and blowing it into Abramović's mouth, after which she breathed a mouthful of carbon dioxide into his mouth. They repeated these actions until both artists almost fell unconscious. During the performance their noses were blocked with cigarette filters to prevent them from breathing in any fresh oxygen, and they wore microphones on their chests to amplify the sound of their accelerating heartbeats. The performance lasted more than fifteen minutes.

DARA BIRNBAUM
1946, New York, New York (US)
Technology / Transformation: Wonder Woman, 1978
Video installation, color, sound, 5 min., 28 sec.

Dara Birnbaum was one of the first video artists to use actual television footage in her work. For *Technology/Transformation: Wonder Woman* she used images from the popular *Wonder Woman* TV series from the 1970s, in which lead character Diana Prince (like Superman) transformed from office clerk to superhero. Birnbaum chopped up the storylines and dialogue from various episodes, leaving only explosions, transformations, and action scenes, which appear in rapid succession. In the background we hear the funk song *Wonder Woman Disco*, from the original soundtrack of the series. The lyrics are full of sexual innuendo, and at the end of the video they scroll up the screen like closing credits.
Birnbaum's video is a harsh critique of the underlying stereotypes in the popular television show. Wonder Woman may have supernatural powers, but she remains a reflection of male fantasy, a prim secretary who changes into a scantily clad heroine. When, halfway through the video, she is captured by her own mirror image, she is unable to free herself. By repeating and slowing down these images, Birnbaum also shows us that it is editing, in particular, that makes television such a hypnotic and seductive medium.

GLOBE SPEELT GEORG BÜCHNER'S
Leonce en Lena

ANTHON BEEKE
1940, Amsterdam (NL)
Leonce en Lena (Leonce and Lena), 1979
Poster, offset and screenprint, 109.8 × 81.4 cm

A designer of advertisements, posters, books, stamps, and magazine covers, Anthon Beeke originally became famous in the Netherlands after the publication of his *Naked Alphabet*, a font consisting of photographs of nude women posing in the shapes of letters. This controversial design was a reaction to the functional *New Alphabet* created by Beeke's former tutor, Wim Crouwel, which was based on computer characters (p. 151). As opposed to Crouwel, who above all valued being informative, Beeke felt that "a poster needs to shock."

This work, *Leonce and Lena*, is based on a satire about a world of boredom and idleness, written by George Büchner in 1836. In the play, Prince Leonce and Princess Lena are promised to each other in an arranged marriage, yet each rebels and escapes this fate – only to end up meeting later by chance, falling in love, and marrying. Beeke depicts the moment the protagonists rediscover each other. The white-painted faces with black makeup refer to the masks worn by Leonce and Lena, but also evoke the black eye patch and heavy makeup worn by lovers Sid and Nancy, the self-destructive punk couple of the 1970s.

CINDY SHERMAN
1954, Glen Ridge, New Jersey (US)
Untitled Film Still #54, 1980
Gelatin silver print, 71.2 × 96.6 cm

This photograph is part of the *Untitled Film Stills* series that Cindy Sherman produced in the period 1977–1980. The black-and-white image appears to come straight from a 1950s film.
Film Still #54 shows a woman in the street, who appears to be rather nervous. The entire series consists of sixty-nine black-and-white photographs of Sherman herself, acting in scenes from imaginary films of her own devising. In depicting a series of typical female characters, Sherman calls into question the image of women and the roles assigned to them.
Sherman always works in series, and she only photographs herself. Disguised as a clown, a femme fatale, or a man with a moustache, she constantly touches upon themes like authenticity, imitation, identification, and stereotyping. Her characters, both seductive and disturbing, invite us to interpret narratives which, though vague, are clearly about gender and role-playing. The fascinating characters from Sherman's costume wardrobe undermine traditional relationships between men and women, as well as stereotypical images of wealth and power.

ANSELM KIEFER
1945, Donaueschingen (DE)
Innenraum (Interior), 1981
Oil, acrylic and paper on canvas, 287.5 × 311 cm,

Anselm Kiefer draws the issues and symbols he uses to examine German history and identity from mythology, history, culture, alchemy, and religion. The main theme of his work is the hole that national socialism left in Germany's cultural traditions. The dark palette and raw materiality of *Innenraum* create an uncomfortable sense of abandonment and decay. The paint is mixed with straw, and the areas of wall between the pilasters are covered with paper painted black. The fire in the foreground consists of fragments of woodcuts. Kiefer often works with different layers and materials, turning his paintings into semi-sculptures. In the 1980s and '90s, when new media, conceptual art, and cool abstraction dominated art, Kiefer's robust, emotionally charged work did not always find favor with critics. Now, however, it is acknowledged that few artists can match his grand vision and ability to find the right balance between a powerful visual idiom and razor-sharp analysis.

NAN GOLDIN
1953, Washington, D.C. (US)
Nan One Month After Being Battered, 1984
Silver dye bleach (Cibachrome), 50 × 60 cm

In order to get a grip on her life, at age eighteen Nan Goldin began photographing her world: the New York punk scene of the 1970s and '80s; a world of drinking, drugs, and sex. She took countless photographs of herself and her friends, often in intimate situations. Together the pictures form "a diary others are allowed to read."
Nan One Month After Being Battered is the climax of the series she named the *Ballad of Sexual Dependency*. Goldin made this raw self-portrait a month after her boyfriend Brian had beaten her so badly she almost lost her sight. With no darkroom to print the photos, she presented the series in the form of a slide show.
The environment in which Goldin found herself was also hit hard by the AIDS virus. "AIDS changed everything in my life. There's life before AIDS, and after AIDS," said Goldin, and she used photography to arm herself against the loss of friends. The *Cookie Portfolio* documents her fifteen-year friendship with Cookie Mueller, who died of AIDS in 1989.
Her diarist approach has influenced many contemporary photographers, including Wolfgang Tillmans. Goldin shows that a photographer does not need technical stunts or impressive subjects to create subtle, meaningful images.

KEITH HARING
1958, Reading, Pennsylvania – 1990, New York, New York (US)
Apartheid, 1984
Acrylic on canvas, 300 × 365 cm,

Keith Haring's gargantuan painting, *Apartheid*, is symptomatic of his well-known activist leanings ignited by the political landscape of the 1980s, a decade featuring murmurings of nuclear warfare, the rise of Reaganomics, and an increase in widespread conservatism. Evidenced in this work in particular is his criticality towards the South African government. Here the black figure is depicted as being much larger than its white counterpart, referring to the irony of the white minority dictating the societal conditions in South Africa. The restraining band around the black figure's neck is not only a symbol of control over the black population, but also a historical reference to slave collars.

During the 1980s this painting was printed on various items, such as t-shirts and mugs, rendering Haring a true "artist of the people," a role which he equally played in his involvement with the gay population during this same period. One of the first artists to openly depict loving relationships between male figures, Haring's works inspired critical reflections on the management of the AIDS crisis in the United States. Although Haring's career was cut short by his premature death from complications of AIDS at age thirty-one, his activist artistic philosophy stills resonates today with various underrepresented and oppressed populations.

MARTIN KIPPENBERGER
1953, Dortmund (DE) – 1997, Vienna (AT)
Drei Hauser mit Schlitzen (Betty Ford Klinik,Stammheim, Judische Grundschule), 1985
Oil, bronze paint and silicone paste on canvas, three parts, each 125 × 150.5 cm, acquired with the generous support of the Mondriaan Fund, the Vereniging Rembrandt and on behalf of the Prins Bernhard Cultuurfonds, thanks to the Titus Fonds of the Vereniging Rembrandt, and the VSBfonds, 2008

Artist and provocateur Martin Kippenberger left behind a hugely varied body of work, ranging from paintings and sculptures to installations and performances. He drew inspiration from many sources, including history, politics, popular culture, and his own life. Kippenberger's work is typical of the 1980s, a time when art was declared dead and there was a prevailing idea that it was impossible to make new and original work. Kippenberger confronted the art world, in particular, and any social inevitability in general.
Drei Häuser mit Schlitzen (Three Houses with Slits) expresses Kippenberger's aversion to institutionalized power. Depicting an American rehabilitation clinic, a German prison for political prisoners, and a Jewish primary school alongside each other, he highlights their similarities. Each is an impregnable fortress in which people are forced to conform to the prevailing norms and values. His paintings are both figurative and abstract, the lyrical expression of coarse brushstrokes clashing with the stripes squeezed directly from the tube onto the canvas. Compared with the serious paintings of his contemporary and fellow German, Anselm Kiefer, Kippenberger's work is much more immediate and confrontational. He liked to break taboos, and would not shrink from deliberate obscenity or absurdity.

DAN FLAVIN
1933, Jamaica, New York – 1996, Riverhead, New York (US)
untitled (to Piet Mondrian through his preferred colors, red, yellow and blue) and *untitled (to Piet Mondrian who lacked green) 2*, 1986, fluorescent light, 1828.8 × 1097.3 cm and 1585 × 731.5 cm, acquired with the generous support of a private donor, the Mondriaan Fund, the Vereniging Rembrandt and its Titus Fonds, 2012

From 1963 onwards, Dan Flavin worked mainly with fluorescent tubes, fittings, and colors. Like the minimalist "sculptors" Carl Andre (p. 159) and Donald Judd (p. 221), he took great care with the relationship between the work and the surrounding space and architecture. Flavin called his interventions "situational art."
In 1968 he began making large installations using light. The two-part installation *untitled (to Piet Mondrian through his preferred colors red, yellow and blue)* and *untitled (to Piet Mondrian who lacked green) 2* was commissioned by Stedelijk director Wim Beeren. Like other installations by Flavin, this work explicitly refers to art history. Flavin regarded Piet Mondrian as his forerunner, because he produced abstract art using only pure colors. Flavin's work in red, yellow, and blue, the primary paint colors used by De Stijl, is a heartfelt tribute to Mondrian. The second, additional installation features green which, though rejected by Mondrian, was vital for Flavin, who worked with light rather than paint. Light consists of the three colors red, blue, and green. Flavin looked at Mondrian's ideas from his own era and perspective, and transformed them into light.

Collection presentation, 2012

JEFF KOONS
1955, York, Pennsylvania (US)
Ushering in Banality, 1988
Wood, paint, 99 × 170 × 89 cm

Ushering in Banality, skillfully carved by hand from limewood, was produced in a series of three. Jeff Koons had it made by master woodcarver Franz Wiser of Tyrol, who also put his signature on the work. It was the flagship display at the *Banality* exhibition in New York, Chicago, and Cologne in 1988, where Koons showed huge figures made of porcelain and painted wood, and in which any distinction between art and kitsch had been abolished. Skillful craftsmanship and banality were designed to seduce the viewer into a sense of carefree enjoyment. Banality, contrary to good taste, is what touches us all most deeply, Koons said. Did he really mean it, or was he simply trying to mock his audience? He maintained this was not mere cynicism, but an attempt to give modern art more allure. Thus, he left serious art lovers struggling with the question of whether this was provocation, irony, sincerity, or all three. *Ushering in Banality* is one of the Stedelijk Museum's most notorious acquisitions.

)ONALD JUDD
928, Excelsior Springs, Missouri – 1994, New York, New York (US)
/ntitled, 1989
\luminum, stove enameled, 150.5 × 750.5 × 165 cm

Donald Judd does not refer to himself a sculptor, preferring to define himself as a "maker of specific objects." In his article "Specific Objects" (1965) he describes how minimalist sculpture attempts to bring about a physical experience in the space. Judd challenged the notion that painting and sculpture refer to things other than themselves, and often create an illusion of space. He wanted to make objects that would function in the here and now. So he removed anything that distracted from the essence, making him one of the most minimalist of all minimal artists.

Having experimented with painting and reliefs, Judd eventually arrived at the box form, which he used for thirty years in all shapes and sizes: as cubes and flattened, open and closed, on the floor and on the wall, separately, and in series. Plain in design and made of industrial materials like galvanized steel, aluminum, and plywood, Judd's boxes have an overwhelming presence. Over the years Judd's work gradually became more colorful. *Untitled,* made in 1989, consists of yellow, red, blue, and turquoise panels attached with bolts. The open boxes invite us to look inside, note their technical perfection, their order and rhythm, and the way they relate to each other, as well as to the wall and the space. *Untitled* proves that a simple form does not necessarily make for a simple experience.

Exhibition *Kramer vs Rietveld: contrasts in the furniture collection*, Stedelijk Museum CS, 2004

091
098
094
099

ETTORE SOTTSASS
1917, Innsbruck (AT) – 2007, Milan (IT)
La torre di Budda (The Tower of Buddha), prototype 1989-1990
Manufactured under the control of Galerie Bruno Bischofberger, Zürich (CH), metal, chipboard, plywood, plastic laminate, MDF, sheet brass, 233 × 120 × 150 cm

At the start of his career Ettore Sottsass was devoted to pure, modern design. But a trip to Asia, during which he fell critically ill, changed Sottsass' outlook on life and design. In India, as he said, he learned about the connective power of stories and the meaning of symbols in society. "If there is one thing that can save us," he said, "it is beauty."
When, confounding all expectations, Sottsass recovered from his illness, he started to design objects with strong ritual qualities. From the mid-1960s, he began to experiment with boldly colored plastic laminates. His vivid color combinations, kitschy motifs, and exuberant shapes and volumes were a radical departure from modernist design, in which color and ornament were taboo. Founding the designers' collective Memphis (named after a Bob Dylan song), Sottsass unleashed a design revolution in the early 1980s. Deliberately flouting "good taste" and drawing inspiration from the entire world and all of history, Memphis helped shape postmodernism. Yet however exuberant Sottsass's designs, they are almost always functional. *La torre di Budda* is a statement about the Western world, which Sottsass believes is obsessed with functionality and technical innovation, but at the same time the object is actually a cupboard.

RINEKE DIJKSTRA
1959, Sittard (NL)
Kołobrzeg, Poland, July 26, 1992, 1992
Chromogenic color print, 93.5 × 74.4 cm

Adolescents on the beach, women who have just given birth, bullfighters after the fight, soldiers on a rigorous training exercise… Rineke Dijkstra became world famous for her photographic portraits of young people at vulnerable moments. The images show little more than the subjects themselves, but their posture, the look in their eyes, and their attire tell the whole story. Most of them stare straight into the camera, and therefore seem to be looking us right in the eye. Every face is unique and at the same time universal, like the insecure adolescent girl in *Kołobrzeg, Poland, July 26, 1992*, who hesitantly adopts an alluring pose. "It's about the interaction between what they choose to show and what they show despite themselves," Dijkstra explained in reference to this series of photographs of adolescents on the beach. Her ability to capture something so personal and indefinable is the essence of her moving and confrontational work. Dijkstra also produces works on video. The Stedelijk collection includes the iconic *The Buzzclub, Liverpool UK/ Mysteryworld, Zaandam NL* (1996–1997), in which she portrays adolescents dancing in their party gear.

bonjour voisin!
mai juin 1994 les élus rencontrent les dionysiens
Mairie de Saint-Denis

MICHEL QUAREZ
1938, Damascus (SY)
Bonjour voisin! (Hello, Neighbor!), 1994
Silkscreen print, 60.2 × 41 cm, gift of the artist, 1994

French graphic designer Michel Quarez makes two types of posters: painterly images with sharp color contrasts, and drawn posters executed in black lines on a white background. Both approaches produce powerful images whose impact comes partly from their humor. The posters have the lighthearted feel of a child's drawing without being in any way childish. In the Paris suburb of Saint-Denis, where Quarez himself lives, his posters promote the local swimming pool or a football tournament, or draw the public's attention to the social issues of AIDS, loitering youths, and integration. His ambition is to produce posters that communicate just as clearly "as road signs on the motorway".
For years Quarez worked as an illustrator, but began designing posters in the 1980s. At first he designed on the computer, but he soon found that he needed the physical movement of a brush across a sheet of paper. Quarez says painting gives him more room to convey his emotions. Interestingly, he not only paints the images on his posters, he also paints the typography, as can clearly be seen on *Bonjour voisin!*
Quarez is a socially engaged designer who also uses his posters in the fight for gay rights or to draw attention to national and international political issues.

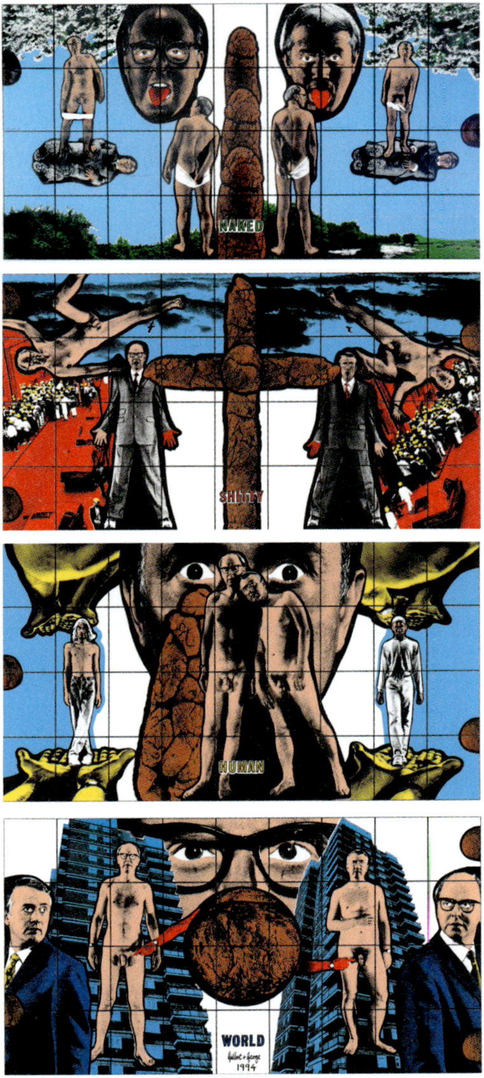
NAKED
SHITTY
HUMAN
WORLD
Gilbert + George
1994

GILBERT & GEORGE
Gilbert Proesch: 1943, San Martino in Badia (IT)
George Passmore: 1942, Plymouth (UK)
Shitty Naked Human World, 1994
Gelatin silver print, colored with dyes, 4 parts, each 338 × 639 cm

Gilbert Proesch and George Passmore met at Saint Martin's School of Art in London in 1967. They have been inseparable ever since. Their debut as a duo was in 1969, with a performance on the steps of the Stedelijk Museum: two stiff, neatly dressed gentlemen with bronze faces and hands, looking around, completely controlled and emotionless. They have been appearing as "living sculptures" ever since, in performances, photographic works, videos, and artists' books.

Art and life are so interwoven for Gilbert & George that there is almost no distinguishing between the two. "First you do your living. And the suffering. Amazing feelings of unhappiness inside. Then you search for pictures to visualize that." Since the 1980s they have been making huge montages of tinted black-and-white photographs with black contours that resemble stained glass windows. The series *Shitty Naked Human World* may appear ridiculous, but the theme is very serious. The combination of excrement, naked bodies, and Christian symbols is an indictment of Christian morality, which constrains people's freedom. "We want our art to be able to speak directly to people," Gilbert & George have said. The message of *Shitty* is unequivocal.

Exhibition *Marcel Wanders: Pinned Up*, 2014

MARCEL WANDERS
1963, Boxtel (NL)
Knotted Chair (Prototype No. 5), 1995/1996
Aramid, carbon fiber, epoxy resin, 71.5 × 53.5 × 71.5 cm

Marcel Wanders caused a furor in 1996 with his *Knotted Chair*, which he created under the auspices of the Dutch design platform Droog Design, in collaboration with the aeronautical department of the Delft University of Technology. The *Knotted Chair* is handmade from aramid cord with a carbon fiber core. The weave was then drenched in epoxy resin and hung to dry. The chair is deceptively light yet exceedingly strong, and despite its unusual shape, it is sturdy enough to sit on. The sober design and the use of new combinations of materials and techniques made the chair a prime example of a style that brought Dutch designers international renown in the final years of the last century. Wanders's method is typified by his out-of-the-box thinking regarding materials and techniques. He chooses traditional techniques like weaving and knotting, and familiar materials like porcelain and wood, but then does something entirely contradictory: he makes flexible macramé rigid and hard porcelain organic. This alienating transformation gives each object a pronounced individual character.
Wanders launched his successful Moooi label in 2001, which has since developed into a springboard for talented international designers. At his studio in Amsterdam, Wanders designs objects and fanciful interiors for hotels, shops, and homes.

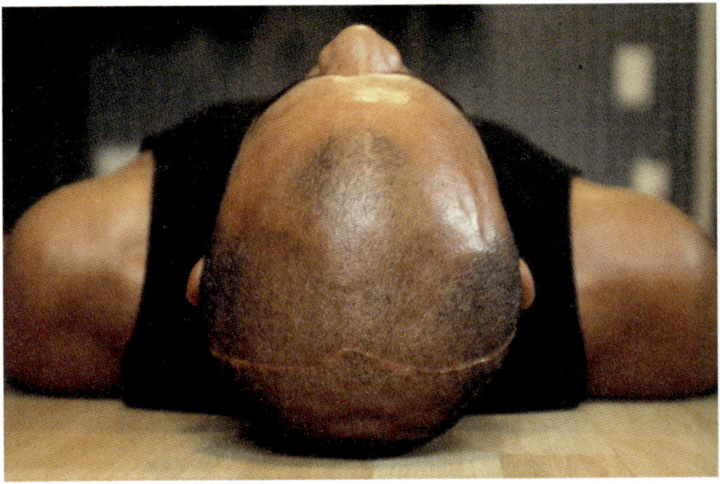

STEVE MCQUEEN
1969, London (UK)
7th November, 2001
Installation with slide projection, transferred to video, color, sound, 23 min., 40 sec.

The head of a man appears. Steve McQueen's cousin, Marcus, is lying on his back in a darkened room. He has a scar across his head, from ear to ear, and in the voice-over he tells the story of a fateful day. On that day, the 7th of November, Marcos was just about to reengage the safety catch after cleaning his pistol, but inadvertently loaded a bullet instead. The gun went off, killing his younger brother. Marcus talks fast and vividly, describing the events and his emotions in an uninterrupted, twenty-three-minute monologue. The picture never changes, but during the course of the account one gradually becomes aware of the association with a body on an autopsy table. What gives McQueen's work its potency is his ability, with just a simple combination of image and sound, to create an extraordinarily emotional work of art. As a director, too, he manages to get right under the skin of his characters, both physically and emotionally. At the same time, he challenges the conventions of the commercial film industry with shocking and confrontational subjects, as in *Hunger* (2008), *Shame* (2011), and *12 Years a Slave* (2013), for which McQueen received an Oscar for Best Picture.

Collection presentation, 2012

GRAYSON PERRY
1960, Chelmsford (UK)
Floating World, 2001
Earthenware, 56 × Ø 44 cm

From a distance there appears to be nothing out of the ordinary about this vase. The shape is familiar, the decoration colorful, and the glaze shines beautifully in the light. But get a little closer and you will see that the surface is littered with car wrecks and bleeding victims. Among them are symbols: a human figure, a coffin, and a phallus. A lifelike gold penis – which for Grayson Perry symbolizes machismo, aggression, and power – adorns the belly of the vase. The contrast between the "safe" form and the shocking content makes for a controversial work. The harsh message is also reflected in the poetic title. The concept of a "floating world" comes from Japanese woodcuts, *ukiyo-e*, which depict nighttime diversions, the company of geishas, and other urban pleasures.

The Stedelijk was an early fan of British potter Grayson Perry's work. Besides pottery, its collection also includes films, a tapestry, and a comic strip. At the opening of *Guerrilla Tactics* in 2002, Perry's alter ego, Claire, dressed in a pale blue child's dress with puffed sleeves, entered the auditorium on the arm of Stedelijk director Rudi Fuchs. A year after this retrospective, Perry was watched by a television audience of millions as he received the Turner Prize as Claire. As non-threatening as Perry's transvestism appears, his work remains biting in its social commentary.

Collection presentation, 2012

SOL LEWITT
1928, Hartford, Connecticut – 2007, New York, New York (US)
Wall Drawing # 1084, 2003
Acrylic, 438 × 1594 cm, gift of the artist and Carl Andre, New York (US), 2003

Sol LeWitt, forerunner of the minimalists and conceptual artists, became famous for his radically different approach to making drawings. Previously, a drawing had generally been a one-off, personal thing, but LeWitt invented a system of notation to record the idea behind his drawings. Just as a composer notates his music in a score, so LeWitt noted down the concept for his drawings in a diagram containing a number of instructions, thus emphasizing the conceptual nature of his art: it is the idea, not the execution, that is unique.
LeWitt produced over 1,200 *Wall Drawings* between 1968 and 2007. In his earliest *Wall Drawings* pencil lines form a thin, gossamer web. In *Wall Drawing #1084* the lines are colored bands some twenty centimeters in width. Nevertheless, all of his wall drawings start with a straight line oriented vertically, horizontally, or diagonally. Like a piece of music, a *Wall Drawing* can be executed several times at different locations, but no two executions are the same.
Wall Drawing #1084 was donated to the Stedelijk Museum in 2003, to mark the departure of director Rudi Fuchs. The gift was a joint initiative of LeWitt and Carl Andre, who owned the concept of this particular *Wall Drawing*.

waar hij de basis zou hebben gelegd
voor de vechtsport.

Ze pakt het wapen op, doodt de schurk...

Dit ben ik, als Koerdisch demonstrant
in een tv-documentaire.

HITO STEYERL
1966, Munich (DE)
November, 2004
Video, color, sound, 25 min., 17 sec., joint acquisition Stedelijk Museum Amsterdam and Van Abbemuseum, Eindhoven (NL), with financial support of the Mondriaan Fund, 2014

November is a fake documentary by Hito Steyerl about her childhood friend, Andrea Wolf. Wolf was an actor, but joined the independence movement of the Kurdistan Workers' Party (PKK) in its armed struggle and was killed in 1998. After her death, her portrait was carried at a protest march in Berlin beside that of Abdullah Öcalan.
In this video Steyerl uses fragments from both cinema films and documentary pictures of Wolf. She has Wolf play many roles: attractive woman, kung fu fighter, martyr for the Kurdish cause, terrorist. By mixing fiction and documentary, Steyerl underlines the fact that, although Wolf chose to join the PKK, she had no control – in this age of digitization and rapid sharing of images – over what happened to her portrait after her death. Steyerl uses methods and resources from the digital world to comment on the current age. She calls our post-revolutionary era, in which there are no longer any universal stories and sweeping change is a thing of the past, "November" (after the revolutionary month of October). The video does not, incidentally, end with Wolf's death, but with her as the sole survivor of the struggle, riding off into the sunset on a motorcycle.

PAUL CHAN
1973, Hong Kong (HK)
6th ~~Light~~, 2007
Installation with video projection, black and white, silent, 15 min., 10 sec., overall dimensions vary with installation, acquired with the generous support of the Mondriaan Fund, 2007

In *The 7 ~~Lights~~*, a series of works on video from 2005 to 2007 that includes this video projection, New York artist Paul Chan combines outmoded computer technology with obscure images. After a slow and tranquil start, *6th ~~Light~~* descends into chaotic darkness. Looming silhouettes of objects are destroyed by unknown forces, and people's shadows dissolve in the dark.
War, politics, sex, and existentialism are prominent themes in Chan's work. He is regarded as a leading representative of a new political art movement in the United States. However, he sees art and politics as two distinct categories that function differently. He therefore likes to keep his life as an activist and his life as an artist separate – something that is not always possible in practice. His activism, for example, is reflected in his performances, printed material, and video documentaries. The video essay *Baghdad in No Particular Order* (2003) includes interviews that Chan conducted in the Iraqi capital just before the American invasion. In 2010 Chan launched the Badlands Unlimited publishing company, which publishes work "that the public has never seen, in accessible formats."

05049

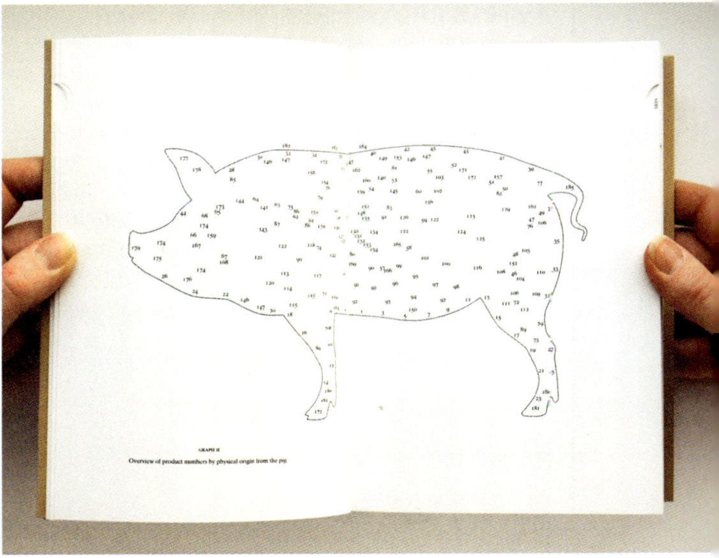
GRAPH II
Overview of product numbers by physical origin from the pig.

CHRISTIEN MEINDERTSMA
1980, Utrecht (NL)
PIG 05049, 2007
Artists' book, 19.5 × 14 cm

Most consumers have no idea of the route a product takes to the store. To trace this invisible production line, designer Christien Meindertsma investigated the "second life" of a single pig: pig 05049. Her three-year study resulted in a book entitled *PIG 05049*, a kind of product catalogue from a single pig.

The 54 kilos of meat, 3 kilos of skin, 15.2 kilos of bones, 14.1 kilos of organs, 5.5 liters of blood, 5.4 kilos of fat, and 6.5 kilos of residual substances taken from the animal were transported across the entire globe. Meindertsma also discovered that pig 05049 provided materials for 185 products, some of them very unexpected, like munitions, medicines, photographic paper, brakes, cigarettes, and cosmetics.

By documenting the "yield" from a single pig, Meindertsma reduced a huge industry – there are twelve million pigs in the Netherlands – to accessible proportions. Parts of the pig and the end products are shown in their actual size. The cover is made of pig's leather, the skin of pig 05049, and attached to it is a copy of pig 05049's bright yellow ear tag.

WIEKI SOMERS
1976, Waalwijk (NL)
Chinese Stools – Made in China, Copied by the Dutch, design 2007,
this copy produced in 2009
Manufactured under the control of Studio Wieki Somers, Rotterdam (NL), stool, cast and lacquered aluminum, 31 × 34 × 22 cm

This red-lacquered aluminum stool originated in Beijing, where Wieki Somers and Dylan van den Berg – who together constitute Studio Wieki Somers – worked for a time. In response to the rapid growth of this metropolis and the Chinese fascination with the "new," Somers deliberately focused on other qualities she observed in daily life there. She became fascinated by the stools and chairs used by security guards, street vendors, and rickshaw drivers. She particularly liked the way the owners would improve, repair, and personalize them. The *Chinese Stools* series brings together many contrasts: East and West, fragile and sturdy, newly made and durable. The chairs and stools have clearly been used for some time, and each has undergone improvised repairs. Both the signature of the maker and the traces of the user are visible. Somers copied the well-used chairs by casting them in aluminum. The original chair was lost in the process, but what remains is an exact replica.

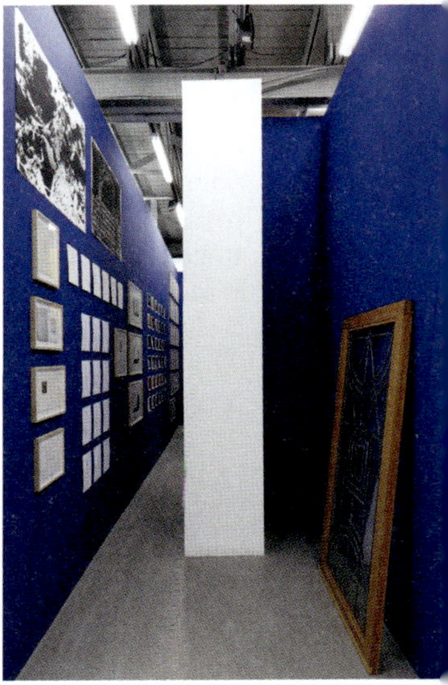

MATT MULLICAN
1951, Santa Monica, California (US)
Subject Driven, 2008
Installation, mixed media, various dimensions

What if the difference between the real and the not-real is not a matter of the laws of nature, but instead a matter of social convention? What if the "real world" is something we learn to inhabit, in interaction with others – a community of belief, passed on from individual to individual, from generation to generation, through the use of symbols? From this point of view, the everyday reality we take for granted is an endless network of signs and meanings, created out of the conventions of those who came before us; a construction that is never quite as cohesive as we would like it to be, which is why we work hard to keep it intact. Matt Mullican is obsessed with this inner process of constructing the world we live in and preserving its stability. In his work he makes these unconscious, interior processes visible and tangible through drawings, sculptures, installations, performances, and readings. In his installation *Subject Driven*, he displays his theories of the "5 Worlds." These five categories include the Elemental World (materials / physical elements), the World Unframed (the everyday relationship to our physical surroundings), the World Framed (the arts and symbolic awareness), the World of Language (signs, coded meanings), and the World of the Subjective (the psychological relationship to the world unframed and framed), each represented by complex systems of colors and symbols. Together they map reality and our own imagination thereof.

Collection presentation, 2016

MARLENE DUMAS
1953, Cape Town (ZA)
Osama, 2010
Oil on canvas, 50 × 41 cm, acquired with the generous support of a private donor, 2012

Looking and being looked at – this is the theme of Marlene Dumas's work, in which she explores the problem of interpretation. Her paintings set out to undermine preconceived ideas and expose inconsistency in them. For Dumas, there is no one single essence, no one single truth.

Dumas often draws inspiration from the photographs in newspapers and magazines in her huge image library. She believes the daily stream of photographic images influences how we look at each other and the world around us. She often chooses images that reflect social norms and values, and then attempts to expose the psychological, social, and political aspects of these images in her paintings.

The controversial piece *Osama* is no exception. This almost sensual portrait of the infamous al-Qaeda leader, with its soft, almost feminine features, confounds our idea of a hardened terrorist, prompting an uncomfortable combination of repugnance and attraction. However, Dumas points out that it is not only pictures that create an image; so too does the written word. She has said of this painting that "the relationship between images and words is very important for me. Would this painting still intrigue us if it weren't for its title?"

WILLEM DE ROOIJ
1969, Beverwijk (NL)
Bouquet VI, 2010
100 black and 100 white tulips, black vase, white base, ca. 180 × 50 × 50 cm, acquired with the generous support of the Mondriaan Fund, 2011

During his time at college, Willem de Rooij was already photographing various bits of the Stedelijk Museum. Each picture showed a piece of skirting board, floor, and two walls. He put the pictures together in a booklet that invited visitors to look at the museum with different eyes. This early project is typical of the way De Rooij explores the power of context over meaning. His entire body of work – consisting of photographs, film, and installations – is about the tension between objects and their meaning or symbolism, which he calls "referential terror," and the limits of authorship. De Rooij has made seven installations featuring flowers since 2002. *Bouquet VI* consists of two hundred tulips of precisely described varieties: a hundred white tulips on one side of the square vase, a hundred black tulips on the other. The number, length, and arrangement of the tulips is identical on each side. None of the black and white tulips are mixed, and each flower is visible in the arrangement. Thanks to the precise description, like a kit, the bouquets can always be installed anew, without any need for the artist's involvement.

STONE MY FACE,
A BOOT
OF THE FUTURE,

BARBARA KRUGER
1945, Newark, New Jersey (US)
Untitled (Past, Present, Future), 2010–2012
Digital print on vinyl, dimensions vary with installation

Identity is a tricky notion. How is it formed by the world around us, and to what is extent does our identity really belong to us? These questions have fueled the work of American artist Barbara Kruger throughout her long career, during which she has utilized combinations of photographs and words to explore the extent of self-dictated identity. Often drawing from mass culture and media, Kruger engages with power structures of representation that can be seen as contributing to the propagation of certain social ideas, often focusing on the objectification of women's bodies, which are viewed as sexual objects in contemporary media culture. In this site-specific installation created for the Stedelijk in 2010, Kruger uses provocative, emotionally charged statements about the way in which human beings regard one another, in order to "speak" loudly and directly to the viewer – a feat she accomplishes within the decorum of a traditional art museum. The phrases Kruger uses in this work – which at times originate from George Orwell's famous dystopic novel *1984* – portray a sense of collectivity by drawing sweeping conclusions that can be applied to each individual viewer, such as the haunting statement, "If you want a picture of the future, imagine a boot stomping on a human face, forever."

ISA GENZKEN
1948, Bad Oldesloe (DE)
Untitled, 2012
Mixed media, various dimensions, gift of the artist, 2016

Isa Genzken's versatile body of work combines themes like physicality, identity, and urban culture. Much of her work is inspired by her life in Berlin and New York. With references to austere Bauhaus architecture and mirrored glass skyscrapers, she touches upon subjects like destruction and construction, access and exclusion, fatalism and utopianism. "Everyone needs at least one window" is one of Genzken's best-known sayings. Windows are eyes, but they also symbolize freedom.

The gleaming pillars of *Untitled* recall skyscrapers with their reflective windows, which allow those inside to look out, while those outside see only themselves. What do you see? Yourself, or the mask you put on for the outside world, like the mannequin in *Untitled*, *Mach Dich hübsch!* is another of Genzken's mantras. "Make yourself lovely. Look for ways of shaping your identity!" Genzken also makes things lovely by combining everyday objects in surprising ways: putting a pair of sunglasses on Nefertiti, or dressing mannequins in her own clothes, exploring the boundary between her private identity and public image.

In one of her rare interviews, Genzken once said, "I want to animate the viewers, hold a mirror up to them," and thus she encourages us to find our own meanings in her work.

ED ATKINS
1982, Oxford (UK)
Ribbons, 2014
Three-channel video installation, color, sound, 13 min., 19 sec., acquired with support of the members of the BankGiro Loterij, 2015

The most important tool for Ed Atkins is his laptop. Using a motion capture camera, animation, and image processing software, he produces videos full of talking heads, body parts, fragments of music, and text animations. The virtual worlds Atkins creates are populated by avatars who speak with his own voice and move like he does. In *Ribbons* we meet Dave, a sentimental, chain-smoking ruffian who drinks far too much and is fast-approaching the edge. “Lonely, lonely,” Dave half-sings, launching into a couplet from Randy Newman’s *I Think It’s Going to Rain Today.* With his hypnotic voice and melancholy eyes, he draws us ever deeper into his universe with his sung and spoken words. Attracting and repelling, beseeching and rejecting, “Dave” plays a sophisticated game with our emotions.
In his videos Atkins creates a world full of illusion, in which the characters are digital fantasies. Paradoxically enough, their virtual bodies make us aware of our own carnality and our life in the physical world. His hyperrealistic virtuality forces us to confront existential questions about the body, love, and mortality.

JON RAFMAN
1981, Montreal (CA)
Still Life (Betamale) – (Ball Pit), 2015
Installation with video projection, color, sound, mixed media, various dimensions, gift of Pierre Trahan, 2017

How does the Internet affect the way we interface with reality? This is the key question addressed in the work of Canadian artist Jon Rafman. The Internet, with all its potential to seduce and alienate, has undeniably caused a rupture in the way people experience the physical world. Rafman explores online subcultures in the manner of an anthropologist. His work is often populated by obsessive characters whose lives are dominated by gaming and other online activities, their hyperindividual mindset balancing somewhere between real life and digital reality. Rafman subtly explores this phenomenon without moralizing or passing judgment. His videos and installations are humorous, melancholic, and full of wonder. The installation *Still Life (Betamale) – (Ball Pit)* consists of a work on video shown above a ball pit the size of a hot tub. Anyone who enters the ball pit is bombarded with images, game graphics, rapidly moving pictures, and low-resolution photographs alternating at breathtaking speed. Avatars also regularly appear. The visual chaos is exhausting to watch, but it is not possible to escape it. Rafman's installation forces us to think about how we should relate to both the physical and virtual world in this digital age.

IRMA BOOM
1960, Lochem (NL)
Hommage à Kelly, 2016
Artists' book, 20.3 × 15.2 cm

Every Irma Boom design begins with paper, glue, and scissors. To determine the correct structure for a book, she first makes a model in miniature. How does the paper feel? How heavy is the book when you pick it up? How does it sit in the hand? How does it smell? Every detail matters. Form and content must be perfectly in balance. Although she works for a variety of clients, *Hommage à Kelly*, an ode to American sculptor Ellsworth Kelly, who died in 2015, was an initiative of Boom herself. Shortly before he died, Boom bought a piece by Kelly: a rectangle divided by a single diagonal line into two quadrilaterals, one black and one white: a form and contra-form. Using Kelly's shapes, Boom designed 160 unique pages using five different colors, then had them folded and bound in such a way that the book eventually had 1,260 different pages. *Hommage à Kelly* was published in an edition of ninety-nine and is a perfect example of how Boom works, always calculating how to make as much as possible with as little as possible.

1895

UNTIL

NOW

1893

1894

1900

1903

1893 The Stedelijk under construction
1894 Construction nearly completed
1900 Period Room
1903 Collection presentation VVHK

THE BEGINNING

The Stedelijk Museum was established thanks to the generosity of private individuals. Sophia Adriana de Bruyn, wealthy widow of Augustus Lopez Suasso, bequeathed her collection and a sum of money to the city. The Van Eeghens, a wealthy banking family, also donated a large sum and a number of artworks to the museum. Construction could begin.

In the late nineteenth century the Museumplein was still an empty field on the outskirts of Amsterdam. Three important cultural buildings were constructed there in just one decade: the Rijksmuseum (1885), the Concertgebouw (1888), and the Stedelijk Museum (1895).

The Stedelijk Museum opened in 1895. It soon became known colloquially as the "Suasso Museum." The new museum displayed a hodgepodge of items, from militia flags to dolls, and from an eighteenth century kitchen to an old pharmacy. But it also housed two important collections of nineteenth century Dutch and French paintings.

1923

1932

1938

1939

1940

1946

1923 Exhibition *Russian Art*
1932 Exhibition *Modern Applied Arts*
1938 Exhibition *Abstract Art*
1939 Poster exhibition
1940 Bunker in the dunes
1946 Commemorative exhibition Piet Mondrian

FROM "SUASSO MUSEUM" TO A MODERN MUSEUM

Slowly but surely the Stedelijk Museum transformed from a nineteenth-century depository into a modern art museum, as its walls gradually became emptier. The feel of modernism – light, air, space – gradually replaced domestic touches like rugs and soft velvet sofas. But the flowers and plants would remain for a while.

The "Museum of Decorative Arts" opened at the Stedelijk on December 15, 1934, displaying furniture, textiles, posters, and glass, with a focus on Dutch items from around 1900. This contrasted sharply with the period rooms, which were still on display.

In 1938 curator (and later director) Willem Sandberg had the red and yellow brick walls painted white and covered with white jute, in order to display modern art to its best advantage. Sandberg was always keen to experiment with different ways of presenting art.

The Stedelijk remained open throughout the Second World War. Its most prized items were taken to a bunker in the Kennemer dunes. Other museums and private collectors also brought their art there for safekeeping. During the German occupation the museum was forced to show "approved" art, but behind the scenes the management silently resisted.

1951

1954

1955

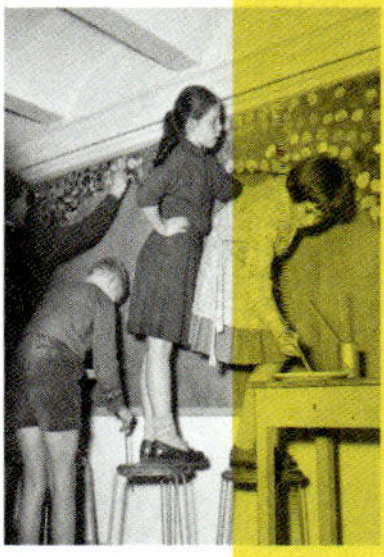

1958

1966

1951 Karel Appel in the Appelbar
1954 The New Wing
1955 Children's workshop
1958 Library
1966 Sculpture garden with fountain by Niki de Saint Phalle

ART ACCESSIBLE TO EVERYONE

After the war the Stedelijk continued to court controversy. The Cobra exhibition of 1949 elicited strong reactions. One newspaper called the artists “daubers, doodlers and varnishers.” But director Sandberg gave Cobra free rein, and even let Karel Appel paint one of the museum’s galleries from floor to ceiling.

Sandberg wanted to make art accessible to everyone. He launched workshops for children at the Stedelijk and introduced the world’s first wireless audio tour. Sandberg’s vision also included a new wing: a light, transparent building where passersby would be able to see the art from the street.

To make things as pleasant as possible for visitors, the museum created a sculpture garden with a pond, a restaurant with a mural by Karel Appel, and a library, its books visible from the restaurant.

1962

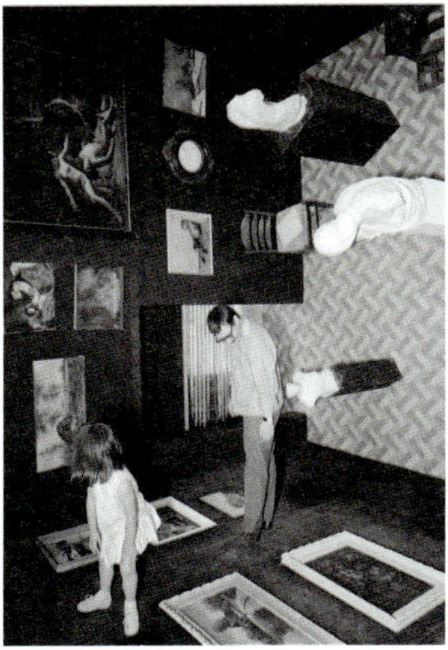

1962

1969

1969

1962 Exhibition *Dylaby*
1962 Exhibition *Nul*
1969 Marinus Boezem, *Bedding Hanging Out of the Windows of the Stedelijk Museum*
1969 Jan Dibbets excavates the corners of the museum

In the 1960s artists were often given a free hand in creating exhibitions, with the Stedelijk functioning as a "place of wonder." In 1961 visitors were entertained by the kinetic sculptures of Jean Tinguely. A year later they were able to lose themselves in the *Dylaby* ("dynamic labyrinth").

During this period, artists often use the Stedelijk as a place for experimentation. In 1962 and 1965, for instance, during exhibitions of the Nul and ZERO movements, the galleries were filled with installations made from things like beer crates and car tires. Edy de Wilde succeeded Sandberg as director in 1963. His policy was to never purchase art more than twenty years old. In these years the art at the Stedelijk is not only young, it is also often born there.

A good example is the 1969 exhibition *Op Losse Schroeven*, which gave an opportunity to question the museum as an "institution." Jan Dibbets literally undermined the museum by excavating the four corners of the building, while Marinus Boezem hung out the laundry.

1969

1970

1973

1978

1969 Gilbert & George on the stairs
1970 Protests by the BBK
1973 Exhibition *Ben Vautier*
1978 John Cage, *Sounday*

In the 1960s and '70s the Stedelijk was the scene of many performances that left a lasting impression. In 1969 Gilbert & George stood for five hours on the steps of the building, as living sculptures made up in gold. "We were born as artists on the steps of the Stedelijk," they said.

In this era of rebellion against the establishment, there was protest both within the museum's walls and outside in the street. In 1970 members of the BBK professional artists' association occupied the museum to publicize their demand for the "democratization of culture." They then marched to the Rijksmuseum. In 1973 Ben Vautier declared in his exhibition that "Art is pretention."

The museum was also regularly home to exemperimental music. In 1978 the American composer and musician John Cage performed his compositions there for a full day. Among the performances were three pieces of chamber music, enhanced by the amplified sound of shells, water, plants, fire, and wind. The performances were broadcast live on Dutch radio.

1983

1985

1986

1987

1989

1983 Daniel Buren, *Caleidscope, a work in situ*
1985 Exhibition *The Luminous Image*
1986 Keith Haring works on his velum
1987 Dan Flavin's installation
1989 Press conference Jeff Koons

In the 1980s the Stedelijk let artists loose on the building itself. At the invitation of Wim Beeren, who succeeded Edy de Wilde in 1985, they made artworks specially for the site, such as Dan Flavin's large neon sculpture in the stairwell, Daniel Buren's vertical stripes above the doorways, and Keith Haring's velum in the grand hallway.

Video was an entirely new medium for artists in the 1980s. In 1984 the Stedelijk Museum organized *The Luminous Image*, a clear signal that it took this new medium seriously.

Controversy is never far away at the Stedelijk. In 1989 Wim Beeren bought Jeff Koons's *Ushering in Banality*. "Beeren's pig" caused a huge furor. "Hideous" and "superkitsch from granny's china cabinet," cried the media.

1989

1991

1994

1997

1989 Endless queues for Kazimir Malevich
1991 Exhibition *Wanderlieder*
1994 Exhibition *Couplet 1*
1997 Rudi Fuchs (l) during the installation of the exhibition *Markus Lüpertz*

After the fall of the Berlin Wall in 1989, there was an upsurge in interest in Russian art, both past and present. The Stedelijk's *Kazimir Malevich* exhibition in 1989 and *The Great Utopia* in 1992 drew huge crowds. This was the first time since the Second World War that Malevich's art had been exhibited on such a large scale in Western Europe.

The Stedelijk also sought out interesting art beyond Western Europe. The search focused mainly on Latin America and Eastern Europe, resulting in the exhibitions *UABC* (Uruguay, Argentina, Brazil, Chile) and *Wanderlieder*, which explored the idea of unification in Europe.

In the 1990s director Rudi Fuchs combined art from entirely different movements, regions, and periods in his presentations. "What visitors really need to accept is that we can't explain everything. At the end of the day there is always an air of secrecy about art." Fuchs also invited Queen Beatrix to curate an exhibition, entitled *A Sovereign Selection* (2000).

2004

2004

2007

2012

2004 Stedelijk Museum CS
2004 Architectural drawing by Benthem Crouwel Architects
2007 Mario Garcia Torres, *Preliminary Sketches from the Past and for the Future (Stedelijk Museum)*
2012 The new building

In the 1990s it became clear that the Stedelijk needed to be renovated and expanded. An international competition was organized to find a design for the extension. Choosing an architect proved a difficult process, however, and in 2003 the museum closed, prior to yet another design competition. By 2004 enough funds had been obtained for the renovation and expansion. The design by Benthem Crouwel Architects, later nicknamed the "bathtub," was chosen in the end.

The Stedelijk moved to temporary quarters, Stedelijk Museum CS, right next to Amsterdam's Central Station, and there continued to stage exhibitions. In the meantime the historic museum building was entirely gutted and carefully renovated. Yet, even then, art continued to be made at the Stedelijk. In 2007 Mexican artist Mario García Torres used the empty building as a backdrop for a new work.

In 2011, when the renovations were complete but work still needed to be done on the new extension, the old section of the building reopened. Art returned to the museum, known for the time being as the Temporary Stedelijk.

The "bathtub" was finally finished in 2012. The Stedelijk could embark on a new phase of its existence, with almost twice as much floor area and more space than ever for exhibitions and its permanent collection.

1

THE BASIS OF ART

1 CLAUDE MONET
La maison à travers les roses (The House among the Roses), 1925–1926, oil on canvas, 66 × 82 cm

To a certain extent, art is a type of manual labor. Until the Renaissance, in fact, art-making was considered artisan work rather than the product of the creative genius we think of today as the visual artist. Yet even in terms of our shifted consideration of the artist figure today, there remains always a certain degree of technical labor in the creation of art objects, whether it be physical construction, digital manufacturing, or even the staging of a performance. Ever present throughout the history of art is the necessity to constantly consider technical properties such as color, line, composition, and harmony. The investigation of color, for instance, was given a boost at the start of the twentieth century, when many painters were inspired by the scientific studies of figures such as Johann Wolfgang von Goethe, who invented the color wheel, and Eugène Chevreul, who proposed that the combination of complementary colors (red/green, violent/yellow, orange/blue) produced the most luminous compositions. Emerging from the fascination with color were styles such as impressionism, one of the first large-scale movements for which the free use of color as a tool to capture space and light was a major departure point. In the unfinished work of Claude Monet, for instance, such attention can be viewed in the way in which the color – and not line or shading – creates the scene depicted (fig. 1). Impressionism, however, also paved the way for movements such

2 ANNA BOCH
Vrouw in landschap (Woman in a landscape), 1890–1892, oil on canvas, 101 × 76 cm

3 THEO VAN RYSSELBERGHE
Marine avec pins et voiliers (Coastal Landscape with Pines and Sailing Ships), 1899, oil on canvas, 46 × 55 cm

4 BARNETT NEWMAN
Cathedra, 1951, oil and acrylic (Magna) on canvas, 243 × 543 cm

as pointillism, a type of painting generated by French painter George Seurat, predicated on the use of small dashes or dots of color as a means of representation. In the work of figures of the Brussels avant-garde group *Les XX*, including Anna Boch (fig. 2) and Theo van Rysselberghe (fig. 3), this style can be viewed in the dispersal of color as an autonomous means of representing light, shadow, space, and physical forms.

Yet despite the seemingly free style of pointillism witnessed in the work of Boch and Van Rysselberghe, compositional balance still maintains a primary role. In Van Rysselberghe's seascape, for instance, the tree, distant land, and horizon line of the water – though depicted only in short brushstrokes rather than true lines – all serve to structure the myriad colors covering the canvas. The principles witnessed in Van Rysselberghe's work, in this case, are not entirely unlike the later work of American painter Barnett Newman, as viewed in his monumental 1951 *Cathedra* (fig. 4). An enormous span of deep, cobalt blue, the monochromatic expanse of the painting is broken up by a vertical area of white canvas showing through, an example of what Newman called "zips." Though categorically not a line, but intended as a spatial feature in itself, the zip serves to also add compositional structure to the color-based surface of the work.

Yet for many artists the two-dimensional surface always referred to an intimate relationship between both color and line. Seen by many as interdependent features in the creation of art objects, color and line were investigated at first largely by abstract painters, who wondered how these

5 PIET MONDRIAN
Compositie met blauw, geel, rood, zwart en grijs (Composition with Blue, Yellow, Red, Black, and Gray), 1922, oil on canvas, 42 × 49 cm

6 WASSILY KANDINSKY
Improvisation 33 (Orient I), oil on canvas, 1913, 88.5 × 100.5 cm

7 FRANCESCO BARZAGHI
Mozes uit het water gered (The Finding of Moses), 1875, marble, 173 × 58 × 67 cm

characteristics could be implemented when naturalistic depiction was no longer the aim. Areas in which these features were explored at length included various artists in the invention of abstraction occurring in the first decades of the twentieth century. In the Netherlands, for instance, the investigation of line and color was headed most prominently by Piet Mondrian. Using only black lines coupled with gray, white, blue, yellow, and red color fields, what distinguished Mondrian's works were that color and line no longer served to represent something else, but were themselves the image (fig. 5). Moreover, Russian-born painter Wassily Kandinsky can be equally seen as inventor of a new way of using line and color in relation to each other. Extremely spiritual in his use of color – believing that certain colors instigated corresponding emotions – Kandinsky's compositions are expressive, passionate, and almost rhythmic in the depiction of shapes, lines, and colors (fig. 6).

The principles of color, line, material, and composition play at least as an important role in the practice of sculpture as they do in painting. The work of Francesco Barzaghi in the late nineteenth century, for instance, is a key example of the use of technical skill to depict a certain narrative. In his 1875 sculpture *The Finding of Moses* (fig. 7), Barzaghi uses various clues to the direct the viewer towards the biblical story of Exodus 2:1–10: the headdress suggests the location of Egypt, the bulrushes refer to the story of Moses, and the woman holding the basket is a clear reference to the person who discovered the baby. Furthermore, the artist's scientific knowledge of

8 RACHEL HARRISON
Amerigo Vespucci, 2006, polystyrene, acrylic paint, mirror with screen print, wood, 219.7 × 78.7 × 73.7 cm

9 PAUL CÉZANNE
La Montagne Sainte-Victoire, ca. 1888, oil on canvas, 54 × 65 cm

the human form is represented in the slight slump of the woman's stance, as if referring to the extra effort needed to stand after picking up the baby. The narrative structure of the work provided by strategic additions is a practice often still seen in contemporary sculpture, for example, in the work of Rachel Harrison. In her wildly colorful *Amerigo Vespucci* from 2006, Harrison depicts an abstract portrait of the famed sixteenth-century explorer who was the first to recognize North and South America as distinct continents that were previously unknown to Europeans, Asians, and Africans (fig. 8). The bumpy, textured surface of the work, however, serves to refer to the transference of measles to the native population from ships' crews such as Vespucci's, which resulted in the deaths of millions of native peoples across the continents of North and South America.
Even in the case of this abstract work, Harrison maintains the use of technical signs to depict the work's narrative meaning.
In addition to the exploration of line, color, and technical details, artists of the modern and contemporary period also grew increasingly interested in space as an independent feature. In the late nineteenth century, for instance, French painter Paul Cézanne became fascinated by perception, to a certain extent in a literal sense by studying the biomechanics of human eyes in their ability to see three-dimensional space. This interest manifests in his ethereal landscapes, such as his work *La Montagne Sainte-Victoire* from ca. 1888, a landscape which appears both naturalistic and three-dimensional, while at the same time is a flat patchwork array of color (fig. 9). The interest in

10 DONALD JUDD
Untitled / Plywood Piece (DJ 26 (84-34)), 1984, plywood (multiply), 260 × 420 × 60 cm

spatial perception later appeared prominently in the contemporary era with the invention of minimalism, a practice emerging in New York in the 1960s. Minimalist sculpture in particular avoided symbolism and self-expression, instead encouraging the creation of crisp, geometric forms which served to transform the physical space they inhabited. Donald Judd's sculpture, for instance, entitled *Untitled / Plywood Piece (DJ 26 (84-34))* consists only of six open-facing wooden cubes hanging on a wall (fig. 10). Yet on further inspection the cubes question the act of hanging an object on the museum wall; unlike paintings, they take up three-dimensional space and transform the physical presence of the wall itself. Featuring the reconsideration of line, color, space, and technical possibilities, the principles of art underwent a major revolution throughout the modern and contemporary periods. Innately fixed to its identity as a physical labor, these principles form the very basis of the creation of artistic objects.

2 EXPRESSIONISM

EXPRESSIONISM: EMOTIONS AND EXPERIENCES TURNED INTO ART

At the start of the twentieth century the term "expressionism" was used for all kinds of modern styles in art, whether it was abstract, cubist, or the vibrant, bold style of painting we nowadays associate with expressionism. It referred to young European artists who challenged the strict rules for art as taught in the many academies. Copying the work of old masters and studying nature, whether in the form of a bowl of fruit or a household object, or in the form of a nude model, formed an integral part of the academy's curriculum. As a result the perfection of line, composition, and color often outranked the expression of emotions or subjective experiences. At the end of the nineteenth century, however, many artists began to deny the rules of the academic style. Impressionist painters such as Claude Monet and Berthe Morisot turned their attention to capturing the essence of the world around them, taking to the streets and going out into nature. The young artists dubbed "expressionists" took that endeavor a step further and turned inwards instead – towards their own thoughts, perceptions, and emotions projected onto the world.
A common trait for those young expressionist artists at the start of the twentieth century was a fierce admiration of the work of Vincent van Gogh. An exhibition of his work at Galerie Bernheim-Jeune in Paris in 1901, a little over ten years after Van Gogh's death in 1890, had

1 VINCENT VAN GOGH
Les bêcheurs (Two Peasants Digging), 1889, oil on canvas, 74 × 93 cm

2 MAURICE DE VLAMINCK
Paysage de Bougival (View of Bougival), 1906, oil on canvas, 60.5 × 73.7 cm

a tremendous impact on the young artists flocking to Paris. Combining extremely bright, opposing colors together to create the most luminous impressions possible, Van Gogh had abandoned the practice of perfectly measuring spatial perspective, used to portray what space literally looked like, and instead chose to freely depict what space felt like. In his 1889 painting *Two Peasants Digging*, for example, the space is not portrayed as expansive and open, as in a typical landscape, but appears instead flattened against the canvas in a swirl of colors and merging of forms (fig. 1). In Paris a group young painters, dubbed *fauves* ("wild beasts"), adopted Van Gogh's use of wild, vibrant colors as a way of expressing light, space, and energy. A good example is the landscape *Paysage de Bouvigal* by the French painter Maurice de Vlaminck (fig. 2). De Vlaminck was a key member of the *fauves*, and *Paysage de Bougival* illustrates the group's use of wild colors, energetic brushstrokes, and a dynamic painting style.
Through traveling exhibitions, organized by artists or small avant-garde galleries, new developments in art traveled quickly. In Germany and Austria young artists also experimented with a style of painting dominated by bold colors, strong lines, and robust shapes, often inspired by art from Africa and Oceania that, in the aftermath of colonial conquests, could be encountered in ethnographic museums in major European cities. Avant-garde artists and gallerists were often avid collectors of these objects. Having no knowledge of, or much interest in their origins, European artists hailed the vitality of these objects and

3 ERICH HECKEL
Stillleben mit Holzfigur (Still Life with Wooden Figure), 1910, paint on burlap, 66.5 × 73 cm

4 ERNST LUDWIG KIRCHNER
Nacktes Mädchen hinter Vorhang (Fränzi) (Nude Behind a Curtain [Fränzi]), 1910–1926, oil on burlap, 120.5 × 90 cm

used African and Oceanic influences as a way to get away from the stifling connection to reality and nature that had defined Western art since the Renaissance (fig. 3). But there were also other important influences, such as Friedrich Nietzsche's thinking on the notion of "vitality." The Dresden modernist collective Die Brücke, for instance, professed the artistic aim of expressing what they called the "vitality of life": the energy associated with youth, sexuality, and individual freedom. Die Brücke artists, including Ernst Ludwig Kirchner and Karl Schmidt-Rottluff, often used vibrant colors and bold brushstrokes to create visually overwhelming compositions. This can be seen particularly in the work of Kirchner, whose colorful and often highly sexualized yet shameless female nudes illustrate the belief of this group of artists in the importance of sexuality as the basis of youthful vitality (fig. 4).
The rise of National Socialism in Germany and consequently the Second World War, however, changed the scene of the European art world drastically. Expressionism was declared degenerate, *entartet*, by the Nazi regime, and many artists fled the war-torn continent to the United States, often forced to leave their work behind, but bringing with them their avant-garde ideas. In post-war Europe the expressionist notion of vitality, now often accompanied by the notion of the *tabula rasa*, the wish for a clean slate, lived on in the bold and colorful art of Cobra (fig. 5). In the United States the basis of expressionism as a mode of painting began to change in the 1950s, as the intention behind the practice shifted from the expression of subjective emotions to the

5 CONSTANT
Birds' Idyll, 1948, oil on canvas, 100 × 55 cm

6 MARK ROTHKO
Untitled (Umber, Blue, Umber, Brown), 1962, paint on canvas, 177 × 137.5 cm

experimentation of painting as a medium. Artists made monumentally scaled works that stood as reflections of their individual psyches – and in doing so, attempted to tap into universal inner sources. Painters began to create increasingly refined ways of expressing particular ideas or emotions, rather than adopting the energetic, loose brushstroke. This can be viewed profoundly in the work of Mark Rothko (fig. 6). The artist was fascinated by mythology and philosophy, and his expressive and carefully composed color fields have been found to instigate a spiritual, transcendent experience in the viewer.

In the 1980s expressionism manifested in the form of a return to painting. Following several decades of experimentation with found materials, ready-mades, and conceptual installations, a number of European artists returned in this period to the monumental canvas and traditional practice of painting. The term "neo-expressionism" was employed to describe the variety of movements emerging in Germany and France involved in this shift. The German painter Anselm Kiefer (fig. 7) and the Austrian Arnulf Rainer employed expressionism as a way of dealing with the history of the Second World War, a topic still difficult to confront, even in the 1980s. Today a painter such as Marlene Dumas employs the painterly gestures of expressionism in her intense, emotionally charged paintings and drawings, which address existentialist themes such as love, death, and desire. Dumas often finds inspiration in newspaper and magazine images from her immense visual archive. She believes that the endless stream of photographic images

7 ANSELM KIEFER
Voyage au bout de la nuit (Journey to the End of the Night), 1990, mixed media, 239 × 750 × 750 cm

8 MARLENE DUMAS,
Magdalena (Manet's Queen / Queen of Spades), 1995, oil on canvas, 300.5 × 101.5 cm

that bombards us every day influences how we see each other and the world around us (fig. 8). Dumas addresses this onslaught by revealing the psychological, social, and political aspects of these images.

From the colorful canvases of Van Gogh to the confronting works of Dumas, expressionism has been employed by artists throughout the modern period as a means of expressing human experience. Created in the face of the strict regulations of the eighteenth- and nineteenth-century academic style, expressionism encompassed the desire to express bliss, sexuality, pain, and fear, tracing the turbulent collective memories and emotions of the twentieth century.

3

ABSTRACT ART

1 PABLO PICASSO
Verre aux chalumeaux (Glass with Straws), 1911, pen, watercolor, and gouache on paper, 29 × 22.6 cm

NEW SHAPES FOR A NEW WORLD – THE INVENTION OF ABSTRACT ART

The invention of abstract art was not the development of a single artist, but rather the result of an exchange of ideas, convictions and artistic solutions within a wide network of artists working simultaneously in many locations, from Paris to Moscow, towards a similar goal: to develop a new art that would match the revolutionary changes taking place in industry, technology, machines, and speed at the beginning of the twentieth century. These artists' movements were nearly universally convinced that abstraction was a more pure and truthful way of representing the modern world. Working concurrently, several international art collectives actively developed a way to visualize this new world, which in some ways had already become reality, but in others still lay in the future. They no longer sought to capture this world through pictorial illusion, but instead chose to use abstract shapes: triangles and squares, lines and cones.

Cubism, developed from 1907 onwards, is considered one of the major steps in the translation of reality to an abstracted composition. Developed by artists such as Georges Braque and Pablo Picasso (fig. 1), cubist works often took standard subjects such as portraits and still-life compositions and transformed them to a nearly unrecognizable extent. These works often have the appearance of a physical subject taken apart and strangely reassembled. Looking

2 DIEGO RIVERA
Stilleven met groen huis (Still Life with Green House), 1917,
oil on canvas, 61 × 46 cm

3 HENRI LAURENS
Bouteille, verre et journal (Bottle, Glass and Newspaper), 1915,
painted wood and metal sheets, 52 × 40.5 × 24 cm

4 KAZIMIR MALEVICH
Suprematist Painting (with black trapezium and red square), 1915,
oil on canvas, 101.5 × 62 cm

closely, the shape of a glass in Picasso's *Glass with Straws* can still be recognized, but the straws have become mere lines. The painting shows many aspects, surfaces, and perspectives of the object simultaneously. Having begun as a style of painting, often using only muted brown and gray tones to depict a variety of subjects, cubism was frequently translated to other styles and forms in the years after 1910, including the use of a more colorful palette adopted by Diego Rivera (fig. 2) and the application of cubism to sculpture, as seen in the work of Henri Laurens (fig. 3).
The abstracted reality of cubism gained increasing momentum in the 1910s in Paris, but it was in St. Petersburg in 1915 that the first truly abstract painting was exhibited. At *The Last Futurist Exhibition of Paintings, 0,10*, Kazimir Malevich premiered his fully abstract suprematist paintings, which were rooted in the depiction of strictly geometric forms: often angular, colored shapes floating in an expanse of white canvas (fig. 4). As Malevich wrote, "In the year 1913, trying desperately to free art from the dead weight of the real world, I took refuge in the form of the square." The term *suprematism* refers to an art based upon "the supremacy of pure artistic feeling" rather than on the visual depiction of objects.

Emerging from the several examples of the foundations of abstraction occurring in Paris and Moscow is the development of abstraction based in the Netherlands. Key among the figures who first brought abstraction to the Netherlands was Piet Mondrian. Influenced initially by the French avant-garde while living in Paris from

5 PIET MONDRIAN
Tableau no. 3: compositie in ovaal (Tableau No. 3: Composition in Oval), 1913, oil on canvas, 94 × 78 cm

6 PIET MONDRIAN
Compositie no. IV, met rood, blauw en geel (Composition No. IV, with Red, Blue, and Yellow), 1929, oil on canvas, 52 × 51.5 cm

1911 until 1914, Mondrian's early works from this period betray the influence of cubism, as can been seen in his 1913 painting *Tableau No. 3: Composition in Oval,* for which he used the motif of a tree as a starting point (fig. 5). In the Netherlands in 1914 – when a short visit became a five-year stay, due to the outbreak of the First World War – Mondrian came into contact with Bart van der Leck and Theo van Doesburg, the latter being the founder of the magazine *De Stijl*. It was in this journal that Mondrian published his theories on a radical transformation of art that would lead to a world in complete harmony, where art and life would be in perfect balance, which Mondrian in turn dubbed "neoplasticism." Mondrian sought a perfect harmony of blue, red, yellow, gray, and white planes of color in his paintings, coupled with strictly horizontal and vertical black (fig. 6). The visual language of De Stijl also manifested in graphic design, objects, and architecture, as evidenced in the furniture of Gerrit Rietveld (p. 45) and designs by Vilmos Huszár (fig. 7).

The first several decades of the twentieth century can undoubtedly be seen as the heyday of abstraction. Following this rapid period of development, however, abstraction began to take on new forms. Following the outbreak of the Second World War, many European artists fled to the United States, among them key figures of the avant-garde, such as Mondrian and Marcel Duchamp. Many artists relocated to New York, where they would reconnect, teach at the art academies, and show their work in

7 VILMOS HUSZÁR
Vignet for De Stijl, design 1917, woodcut, 24.6 × 18.4 cm

8 BARNETT NEWMAN
Right Here, 1954, oil on cotton, 127.5 × 89.5 cm

New York galleries such as the one run by Peggy Guggenheim. In the 1950s abstraction acquired a new purpose in New York. No longer aimed at radical transformation or utopian visions of the future, American artists such as Lee Krasner, Barnett Newman, and Willem de Kooning added the subjective human experience to their emotionally charged, abstract paintings. They succeeded in producing works which were both abstract and highly emotive, creating a profound impression in which emotion itself became the subject (fig. 8).

From the 1960s onward these expressive forms gave way to increasingly "cool" abstraction, which meant that artists turned their attention more and more to the medium of painting itself – to the flat surface of the picture plane, and to paint, line, and color. Form and process became the subject of their work, and references to the world outside the canvas, or utopian visions of the future, seem to have become obsolete. Nevertheless, the result can be as abstract and overwhelming as one of Newman's large canvases, or as proven by Sol LeWitt's *Wall Drawing #1084* (fig. 9). Executed by assistants according to instructions written down by the artist, this large mural makes quite an impression on the viewer. Although his work is very abstract, and in some ways signals a democratization of art which would have been approved by the Russian avant-gardists, LeWitt's wall drawing lacks claim to a universal experience or emotion: "Different people will understand the same thing in a different way," LeWitt said.

9 SOL LEWITT
Wall Drawing #1084, 2003, acrylic on wall, 438 × 1594 cm

From its very inception, abstraction has been a way of accessing an idea which is beyond its realistic visual depiction. As a result, abstract forms today evidence the development of deep philosophies, expressions of emotion, and the political utopianism that exists in the history of twentieth-century art. Illustrating what real objects are unable to represent, abstraction is a way of striving towards a higher truth by means of visual form.

SCRAPS WASTE JUNK

4

1 KURT SCHWITTERS
Ohne Titel (TEZ), 1924/1927, collage, oil, 21.4 × 16.5 cm

In 1917, for the exhibition of the Society of Independent Artists in New York, Marcel Duchamp submitted a sculpture under the pseudonym "R. Mutt," a ceramic object none other than a urinal turned on its side. With this work, art for the first time no longer had to consist exclusively of artistic materials, subsequently rendering new connections between "high" and "low" culture, offering experiments in materiality, and bringing a new sense of reality into artistic practice. Duchamp's groundbreaking submission played an extremely influential role in modernist practices emerging in the years following, having transformed an everyday object into art with one simple gesture. But Duchamp was not the only artist experimenting with lifting objects from their "mundane" existence and transferring them into artworks. One of the leading practitioners was German artist Kurt Schwitters. In the 1920s he began combining all sorts of unusual materials into his collages: he attached newspaper clippings, candy wrappers, and other debris to the surface of his works. In this way reality was quite literally added to a two-dimensional artwork, which until then had mostly been an imitation or interpretation of reality. In his 1924 composition, *Untitled* (fig. 1), we see oil paint, paper surfaces, advertisements, and what appear to be large typographic letters, all layered upon one another – appropriated materials united within a single composition.

2 JEAN TINGUELY
Balouba bleu (Blue Baluba), 1962, oil drum, scrap iron, plastic duck, electric motor, 200 × Ø 76 cm

In the mid-twentieth century the members of the nouveau réalistes collective, founded in Paris in 1960, used found objects to bridge the gap between art and life. They believed that art should focus on the urban, industrialized modern world, in which advertising and mass-produced items were now such an important part. The nouveaux réalistes used everyday and found objects as a means of returning to a reality missing from what they deemed "high art" of the time: abstract painting, which aspired to express the sublime or enable a spiritual experience. Works by the nouveau réalistes were often daring, unpredictable, and even funny, creating a new relationship with their immediate reality through participation, laughter, and unexpected outcomes.
Swiss artists Daniel Spoerri and Jean Tinguely were the most popular artists of the nouveau réalistes movement, and worked alongside fellow members such as Niki de Saint Phalle, Yves Klein, Arman, and Martial Raysse. Tinguely, best known for his mechanized sculptures, often used found objects, and at times even trash, in the construction of his contraptions, as seen in his 1962 *Blue Baluba* (fig. 2). Spoerri, on the other hand, had an even more extreme interpretation of the use of found or everyday objects in his "snare-pictures": dirty plates, silverware, and even a half-empty pack of cigarettes are attached to a wooden surface and displayed horizontally on the wall, like a picture. Such works came into being during the festive opening of the pop-up restaurant Spoerri organized in the City Galerie in Zürich on September 25, 1965. The invited guests were asked to bring their own plates and cutlery,

3 DANIEL SPOERRI
Table from the City Galerie Restaurant (from the series: *Restaurants*), 1965, mixed media, 120 × 120 × 40 cm

4 LEE BONTECOU
Untitled, 1961, steel, canvas, velours, leather, copper wire, soot, paint, 136 × 188.5 × 37 cm

and were served by art critics. Following the dinner, Spoerri glued everything that remained to the tabletop, in order to later mount it on the wall. In this way he transformed a random array of everyday objects and scraps into a still life, fixed for eternity in the moment the artist decided to do something with them. Spoerri would call these works a *tranche de vie* – a slice of life (fig. 3).

The use of found objects also enabled artists to use very contemporary materials, directly connected to the time and world in which they were made. A great example is the work of American sculptor Lee Bontecou (fig. 4), who despite critics' attempts to associate her with movements such as minimalism, feminism, and expressionism, defies all categorization. Bontecou's organic-looking sculptures are informed namely by a combination of her fascinations, which include architecture, technology, recycled materials, and nature. In her work she frequently combined welded metal frames with pieces of recycled canvas, often from mail bags and conveyer belts found in the laundry situated below her studio. The combination of steel structures, soft materials, and the rhythm of the forms ensures that Bontecou's work invokes all kinds of associations, without specifically referring to anything. The mysterious dark holes amplify this sense of indefiniteness. Bontecou has said that her art responds to the historical moment in which it was created: "I wish my work to represent or to be a part of my time… I want them to be things and facts inside us – from war to the wonders of the space age."

5 DAMIEN HIRST
Waste, 1994, glass, steel, paper, fabric, plastic, 160.5 × 214 × 107.5 cm

6 WIEKI SOMERS
Chinese Stools – Made in China, Copied by the Dutch, design 2007, production 2009, cast and lacquered aluminum, various dimensions, manufactured under the control of Studio Wieki Somers, Rotterdam (NL)

Throughout the later decades of the twentieth century, artists continued to use found objects, yet often this use pertained increasingly as a tool for social engagement and criticism. Damien Hirst, for instance, one of the most prominent contemporary artists in Great Britain, often used trash or found objects in works dealing with fetishism and consumerism. In his 1994 sculpture, *Waste* (fig. 5), Hirst placed hospital trash into a glass case, ensuring that the rubbish can be properly inspected by the viewer. The irony of this work is that the objects in the case are in fact not trash, but unused everyday hospital products which Hirst has crumpled and made to look like garbage. By doing so, Hirst calls attention to the speed at which objects are named trash in our world today and the carelessness with which waste is treated.

Currently, many artists continue to use found objects as a means of exploring the world. As direct indicators of commerce, society, and relationships, physical objects serve as investigative tools towards contemporary life. Dutch designer Wieki Somers, for instance, uses furniture pieces considered unremarkable as departure points for an investigation of their tradition, use, and aesthetic value. During a trip to Beijing in 2007, Somers came across a variety of stools and chairs produced by craftsmen and traditional workshops for everyday use in Chinese society (fig. 6). Fascinated by these common yet highly aesthetic and professionalized objects, Somers cast a variety of them in aluminum and recreated them in bright colors. In this sense, Somers also uses everyday objects to reflect on the

7 MESCHAC GABA
Diamants Indigènes, 2008, wooden suitcase, glass, watches with fake diamonds, 65 × 50 × 7 cm

relationship between East and West, exposing the hidden beauty of everyday Chinese furniture at the same time. While it is commonly thought that Chinese designs often stem from European or Western objects, Somers reverses that relationship.
Similarly, Beninese artist Meschac Gaba equally uses everyday objects to reflect on the power dynamic seen in the relationship between East and West (fig. 7). In particular, his 2008 sculpture *Diamants Indigenes* depicts a framed glass case showing a series of cheaply made watches containing false diamonds, referring to knock-off items sold by African street vendors. Referring to the transfer of goods in the area viewed as the Third World, Gaba calls attention attend to objects of value and their role in the globalized system.
Whether radical, humorous, or socially critical, the use of found and everyday objects has played a major role in the history of modern and contemporary art. Through the employment of objects such as trash, furniture, and cheaply made goods, art from the twentieth century until today no longer exists only of traditional materials, but rather generates continuously new ideas and meanings by inserting everyday life into the art object.

5 APPROPRIATION ART

1 ANDY WARHOL
Campbell's Andy Warhol Institute of Contemporary Art, Boston, 1966, silkscreen print, 49 × 43.5 cm

2 KURT SCHWITTERS
Eine Ichzeichnung, 1935, collage, 24.8 × 19.8 cm

WHOSE IMAGE IS IT ANYWAY? APPROPRIATION ART

Appropriation refers to the presence of an image, idea, or narrative in an artwork which is not invented by the actual artist. Separated from their original context, appropriated materials function in modern and contemporary art as tools by which to bring new meaning to old ideas, through combinations that challenge our preconceived notions of art, creativity, and the world around us. The appropriation of images in art has a long history. From the cubist collages of Picasso and Georges Braque, or Kurt Schwitters's Merz works and Andy Warhol's soup cans, using familiar or popular imagery and representing it in a new work has been around for a long time (fig. 1). The inception of appropriation in modern art was influenced largely by the emergence of collage as an artistic practice, when artists started to use everyday materials such as newspapers and advertisements, as seen in the works of many cubists as well as Dada (fig. 2). Perhaps most canonical in the practice of appropriation is Marcel Duchamp, master of transforming the meaning of an object through artistic manipulation. Initially instigated by his richly ironic 1917 *Fountain,* a urinal turned upside down and termed not only a "fountain," but also a work of art, this work signals the invention of the ready-made: a work of art not originating from the labor of the artist's own hands, but one which is recontextualized within an artistic framework. Duchamp's later

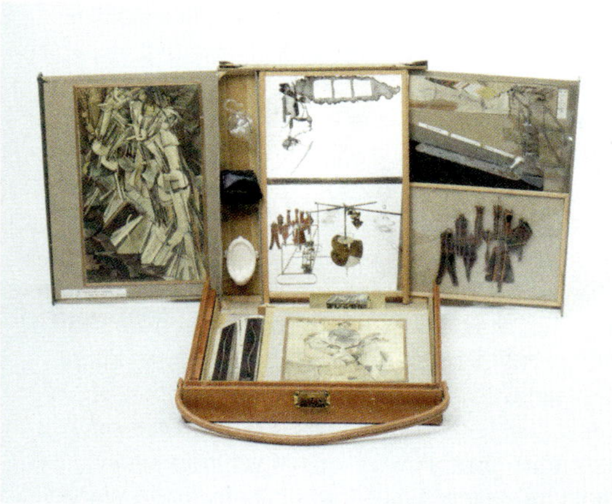

3 MARCEL DUCHAMP
La boîte-en-valise (Box in a Valise), 1936–1949, mixed media, dimensions vary with installation

work continued to reflect appropriation techniques in constantly reinvented ways. His work *La boîte-en-valise* is a small leather carrying case which opens up into a scaled-down exhibition of his work, complete with folding frames and consisting of sixty-nine miniature replicas and reproductions of his work, including a mini-urinal and depictions of famous works, such as *The Large Glass* and *Nude Descending a Staircase* (fig. 3). The case fits very well within the oeuvre of Duchamp, who decided that a work of art no longer had to be unique or made by the artist him- or herself. This prompted much discussion about the significance of an "original" artwork. His case full of reproductions, with its first "deluxe" edition of twenty copies, echoes this development.

In the wake of the first experiments in appropriation occurring in the early twentieth century, European and American artists of the 1960s implemented these notions within the shifting tides of contemporary practice. In this period artists often used everyday, appropriated materials in order to question the status of art as a symbol of "high culture." Two key figures in this sense were pop artists Jasper Johns and Robert Rauschenberg. Both New York-based artists, Johns and Rauschenberg were best known for redefining the notion of the flat surface through their "combined paintings": canvases whose surfaces they disturbed by attaching to them appropriated materials (fig. 4). From items as innocent as small texts and scraps of newspaper, to large objects such as chairs, casts of body parts, household items, and even trash, the

4 JASPER JOHNS
Untitled, 1964–1965, oil on canvas, broom and rulers, 182.5 × 478 cm

5 ROBERT RAUSCHENBERG
Charlene, 1954, assemblage on canvas, 225 × 321 × 11.5 cm

colorful works of Johns and Rauschenberg were littered with three-dimensional items. One of the best examples of such a work is Rauschenberg's 1954 *Charlene*, (fig. 5) a "combined painting" upon which Rauschenberg attached a light bulb, fabric swatches, and even an umbrella. The space in which *Charlene* hangs has a great impact on the piece: the large mirror reflects the area surrounding the painting and the wall behind the painting is visible through a cutout to the left of the umbrella. About his use of objects from the real world, Rauschenberg stated, "I don't want a painting to look like something it isn't, I want it to look like something it is." Johns and Rauschenberg transformed the meaning of the flat surface and introduced the notion that painting need not be confined to the boundaries of traditional "high art."

Pop art, however, was not only focused on the relationship between "high" and "low" culture, but often reflected critically on the emergence of mass media and consumerist culture, which had become deeply culturally embedded in the post-war period. As Andy Warhol said, "Pop artists did images that anyone walking down the street would recognize in a split second – comics, picnic tables, men's pants, celebrities, refrigerators, Coke bottles." Working in the wake of figures like Johns and Rauschenberg, American sculptor Jeff Koons is most often associated with a critical evaluation of consumerist culture through the use of appropriation techniques. In his 1988 sculpture *Ushering in Banality*, for instance, Koons presents an enormous re-creation of an ornamental figurine. Changing almost nothing

6 TADANORI YOKOO
Beams, 1997, silkscreen print, 103 × 72.7 cm

from the original trinket, the scale used to depict the object is jarring, forcing one to consider the presence of kitsch and useless items found in popular culture. A key figure who continues to reflect on this facet of pop today is Japanese graphic designer and printmaker Tadanori Yokoo. Yokoo's work utilizes mass-media advertisements and newsreel photographs to create multilayered images. Often combining psychedelic colors with traditional Japanese print-style images, Yokoo contrasts historical Japanese artistic practice with mass consumer and media culture, all with a sense of dark irony. In his 1997 poster, *Beams*, surrealism clashes with reality, advertisement with aesthetics (fig. 6).

In recent decades the appropriation of images and ideas has instigated a variety of intriguing questions about the nature of art itself. For instance, to what extent is "originality" important in contemporary practice? What does it mean to be the "author" of an artwork? Among the artists whose works are driven by these question is Louise Lawler, whose oeuvre consists of manipulated photographs and reproductions of the interior views of galleries and museum installations (fig. 7). In her 1995 work, *Untitled (Recent)*, she depicts a photograph of a room in the Stedelijk Museum curated by then-director Rudi Fuchs and on display from 1993 to 1995, viewable through a crystal half-sphere which distorts the photograph below (fig. 8). Presenting minimally manipulated documentary photography as an artwork, Lawler pushes her works to the limits of traditional understandings of "creativity" and "originality" – the very qualities which have

7 LOUISE LAWLER
Produced in 1988, Purchased in 1989; Produced in 1989, Purchased in 1993 (adjusted to fit), 1995/2010, photograph on vinyl, dimensions vary with installation

8 LOUISE LAWLER
Untitled (Recent), 1995, crystal, cibachrome, and felt, 118 × 30.5 × 30.5 cm

historically constituted an artwork – and therefore accomplishes new ideas and meanings through the act of appropriation.
Unlike the invention of new images, the practice of appropriation allows artists to rework and transform the preconceived ideas about art, its role in the world around us, and its relation to historical notions of art-making. Pushing the boundaries of artistic practice to its very limits, appropriation tests what we believe we know about creativity in the contemporary world.

6 WHERE DID THE ART GO?

1 JAN DIBBETS
Museumsokkel met 4 hoeken van 90° (Museum Plinth With Four Corners at an Angle of 90°), 1969

In the mid-twentieth century the art object began to disappear. In reaction to the age of growing consumerism, technological progress, and standardization, artists began to reject the notion of the artwork as a unique product of artistic genius by creating works which were repeatable, required little construction, and existed increasingly more as an idea than an object. Termed "conceptual art," this new type of art-making revolutionized the artist and artwork alike, signaling a new age in artistic practice.
The Stedelijk Museum in particular played an important role during the emergence of conceptual art, exemplified most clearly in the 1969 exhibition *Op Losse Schroeven: Situaties en Cryptostructuren* (loosely translated as *Square Pegs in Round Holes: Situations and Cryptostructures*). Featuring international figures such as Hanne Darboven and Bruce Nauman, as well as Dutch conceptual artists such as Jan Dibbets and Ger van Elk, this exhibition was radical and experimental, consisting of simply constructed works and spatial installations termed "situations." A key example in this show was *Museum Plinth With Four Corners at an Angle of 90°* by Jan Dibbets, for which the artist hollowed out the earth at several corners of the museum, thereby exposing the foundation and suggesting its role as a colossal podium for the museum structure (fig. 1). In addition, Ger van Elk erected an immense curtain spanning the

2 GER VAN ELK
Apparatus Scalas Dividens, 1968, mixed media, 113 × 40 × 210 cm

monumental main staircase of the Stedelijk, splitting it into two aisles more similarly organized to roadway traffic than a grand architectural feature (fig. 2). This groundbreaking exhibition staged by then-curator and later director Wim Beeren paved the way for conceptual art in the Netherlands and introduced the public to a reinvented means of artistic production. Corresponding to the decreasingly material properties of the art object was the induction of language as a tool to convey the concept at work, make a joke, or question the object to which it refers – at times performing all three simultaneously. A good example is Joseph Kosuth's *Five Fives*. This sculptural work consists of written words in neon lettering, forcing the viewer to question whether the work should be understood visually or linguistically, as sculpture or as text. This double meaning was also applied to other mediums, such as artists' books, posters, and works on paper. In the 1969 work of Japanese artist On Kawara, entitled *One Million Years*, (fig. 3) the artist records two million years – the one million prior to 1969 and the one million which will occur thereafter. With each page describing five hundred years, a human life barely takes up one fifth of a page, and humanity in general occupies only a minute fraction of the entire book. Existential and contemplative, this work exists both as a conceptual way of rethinking human presence on the earth and as an aesthetic object in which the endless numbers on each page present nonetheless a striking aesthetic beauty.

As the definition of the artwork as a creative imprint of the artist began to disappear, along with the object itself, through the creation of

3 ON KAWARA
One Million Years, 1999, artist's book, 16.2 × 11.8 × 9.1 cm

repeatable works and projects, so did the authority of the artist as the beloved genius figure. This newly developed attitude towards what can be termed simply "authorship" is perhaps best characterized in the work of Stanley Brouwn, one of the most elusive artists of the twentieth century who was, in a quite literal sense, difficult to place. He would never show up at exhibition openings and rarely allowed photo reproductions of his works to be published in books, while photographs of the artist himself are few and far between. All that is commonly known is that he was born in 1935 in Paramaribo, Suriname, that he died in Amsterdam in 2017, and that he was an artist, of course. One of his most well-known projects is entitled *This way Brouwn*, and consists of a series of seemingly abstract drawings depicting directions drawn by random pedestrians after Brouwn had requested help in reaching a certain point in the city. The drawing, marked by the passersby and stamped with the notation "this way Brouwn," thereby removes Brouwn as the typical creative "author" figure and renders a work whose meaning is dictated by organic interaction in a public space, clearly adhering in this instance to the principles of conceptual art. In addition to Brouwn, who in a very literal sense removed the author from the equation, many conceptual artists attempted to deconstruct authorship in a more ideological sense. Canonical among examples of this aim was American artist Seth Siegelaub's 1968 *Xerox Book,* a publication consisting of works on paper from fellow artists such as Lawrence Weiner, Sol LeWitt, and Robert Barry (fig. 4). The initial aim of this work was to

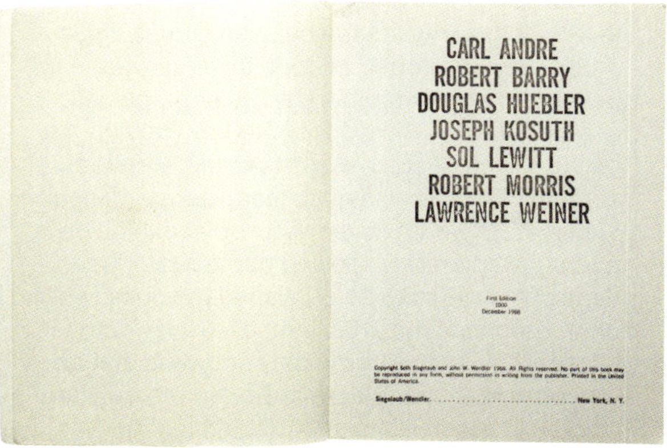

4 SETH SIEGELAUB
Untitled (Xerox Book), 1968, offset lithography, 28 21.4 cm

use a Xerox copy machine to cheaply reproduce and distribute the manual. Yet even the Xerox copier proved too expensive, and Siegelaub eventually used offset printing instead. Though on the surface it seems a bit absurd, Siegelaub's *Xerox Book* manifestly signaled a desire to escape the definition of art as something unique, valuable, and tied to a specific author. Rather, the role played by reproduction techniques in this work exercises the notion of art as a cheaply made, unexceptional, and authorless object of autonomous meaning. As the normative boundaries of materiality in artistic practice continued to be loosened through conceptual art, Land art also emerged as a means of rendering art from natural, found objects. At times consisting of outdoor sculptures rendered from such objects, Land art can also be viewed as the inspiration behind artists who brought natural materials into the museum as independent art objects, resulting in the continued critique of the role of the artist as "creator." Emerging mainly in the work of American artists, the latter practice was promoted in large part by Richard Long, an artist who created sculptural installations from natural materials such as rocks. In his 1978 work *Bluestone Circle* (fig. 5), Long arranged ninety-six stones on the floor in a randomly distributed fashion. Without any of the stones touching one another, the final spatial arrangement of the installation was coupled with an illustrated document describing the concept of the work, thereby continuously referring to the process rather than result.

From performances to installations to wall drawings, where does art exist when placed under the

5 RICHARD LONG
Bluestone Circle, 1978, bluestone, 14.5 × Ø 486 cm

conditions of conceptualism? Witnessed through the impulse of orienting an artwork towards its underlying idea rather than material qualities, the boundaries of the art object were continuously loosened throughout the mid- to late-twentieth century, molding the word "art" into a variety of new and experimental meanings.

7

COUNTER CULTURE

PROTESTS AGAINST THE ESTABLISHMENT: ART AND COUNTERCULTURE

Counterculture, if contextualized generally, can be understood as the common desire to disrupt the otherwise accepted status quo. Yet what does this mean in terms of artistic practice? How have projects in design, photography, performance, and visual arts transformed our understanding of revolution and what it means to reject the status quo? Turning order into chaos, countercultural movements allow for a glimpse into a time in which creativity – and sometimes even absurdity – was used as a tool for the reconsideration of the world as we know it. Many artists embraced the magazine as a fitting vehicle for their theories and ideas; easily shipped by mail, it was an effective way to promote and disseminate ideas, as well as the art itself, in many cases.

Though counterculture has existed to some degree throughout the modern era, the word itself is most often associated with the social revolution which occurred in the wake the Second World War. Amsterdam, city of freedom, magic, sex, and drugs, was at the center of countercultural movements in the 1960s. Although the atmosphere in the city could be grim because of confrontations between protesters and the police, a unique, alternative youth culture blossomed, in which "the provocation" was an important method: an often playful, anarchistic manner of undermining authority. The activities of contemporary artists during this period fueled the experimental

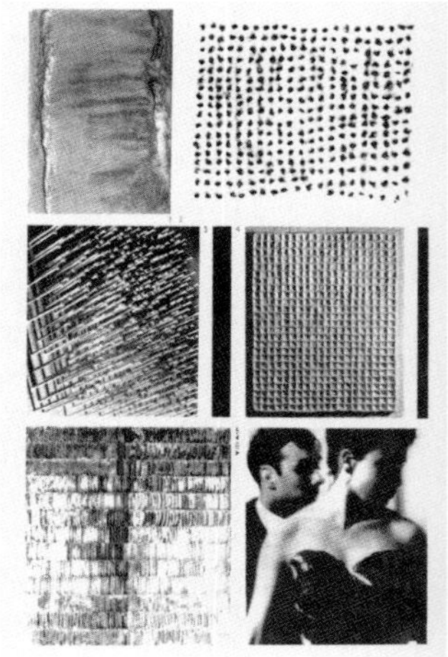

1 ZERO demonstration in Arnhem (NL), 1961. Among the various spectators in attendance are Stanley Brouwn, Rik van Bentum, Franck Gribling, Peter Iden, Rochus Kowallek, Heinz Mack, Friedrich-Karl von Oppeln, Henk Peeters, Otto Piene, and Günther Uecker.

2 ARMANDO, HENK PEETERS, HERMAN DE VRIES
Magazine *nul = 0* (Zero = 0), autotype, letterpress, typescript,
27.6 × 22 × 1.8 cm

mood in the city, particularly in the case of the Dutch Nul group, which had joined forces with German ZERO in 1960. Consisting of members from Germany, the Netherlands, France, Italy, and Japan, the Nul group staged raucous parties, demonstrations, and performances as revolutionary means of promoting their art (fig. 1). In doing so, they not only reinforced the revolutionary urge towards social chaos occurring throughout their urban setting, but also redefined the status quo of the art world by throwing traditional means of exhibition-making into chaos. Shortly after the publication of the third edition of *ZERO* magazine in 1961, Dutch artists Henk Peeters, Armando, and herman de vries set up their own magazine, *nul = 0* (fig. 2). With their magazines, often published in more than one language to further international communication, the artists took control over the discourse on their art.

In this spirit of the late sixties – the student revolts, the experiments in art, literature, and painting – artist, collector, and dealer William Copley founded his S.M.S. studio in New York. Together with artist Dmitri Petrov, he initiated the magazine/multiple/portfolio *S.M.S (Shit Must Stop)* – a title referring to the punch line of a dirty joke, but also to artists' dissatisfaction with what they felt was a corrupt art market and a highly hierarchical museum establishment (fig. 3). In a letter to his friend, the artist Joseph Cornell, Copley described *S.M.S.*'s mission:

"As you will see it is a mixture of many things. We are not trying to push any kind of art but rather to suggest how many different ways ideas can go. So we include the old and the new in a context

3 BILL COPLEY
S.M.S. (Shit Must Stop), 1968, 6 portfolios with 70 original multiples, 18 × 33 cm

that is meant above all to surprise and make of the box itself a sort of adult joy." Over sixty artists were invited to contribute an artwork, which was consequently exactly replicated and distributed to subscribers through the mail in printed boxed envelopes. Participants included, among others, Meret Oppenheim, Yoko Ono, Bruce Nauman, Claes Oldenburg, Roy Lichtenstein, and Terry Riley, and subscribers could encounter anything upon opening their envelope, from a recording of Nauman's footsteps or a Chinese fortune game, to a set of plastic bags containing screws, glue, Plexiglas, and several other items, in order to assemble an artwork by Arman. Copley envisioned *S.M.S.* as a populist, utopian platform that bypassed the established hierarchy of the art world. It was founded on a democratized approach to the arts, bringing together poetry, sound, graphic design, and visual art. The principle of equality also applied to financial matters, with all participants receiving one hundred dollars for their contributions.

As counterculture continued to develop in the 1960s, it was not only daily activities that were reimagined by new ways of thinking, but also the very structures of contemporary life. Capitalism, class structures, and the traditional family unit began to be reexamined by alternative-thinking groups of artists, musicians, and writers, figures who eventually included the founding members of the Situationist International movement, founded by Dutch artist, theorist, and architect Constant Nieuwenhuys. Having already gained recognition as a Cobra artist, between the years 1956–1974

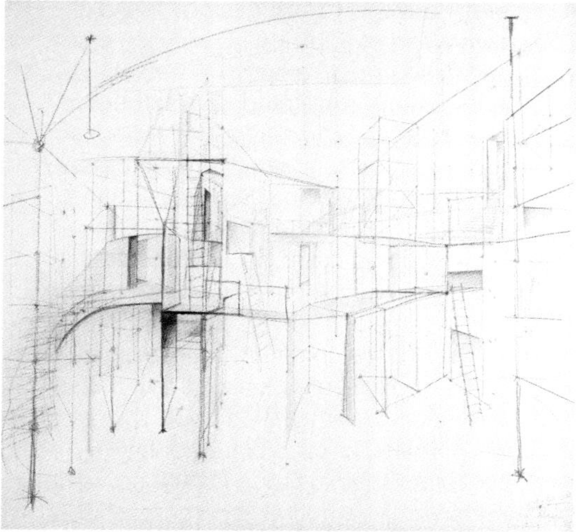

4 CONSTANT
Mobile Labyrinth E.S.R. New Babylon, 1966, pencil on paper, 127.3 × 140 cm

he created countless versions of his imaginary labyrinthine city of *New Babylon* (fig. 4). Rejecting the dogmatic structures of capitalist society, *New Babylon* would be a place where the traditional family unit would be dissolved and its residents could be free to exercise their creative abilities through experiments in games and technology. With living spaces existing above the contemporary city, *New Babylon* would transcend both literally and figuratively the restrictions of everyday life. After *Plans for New Babylon* was exhibited in the Stedelijk Museum in 1959, Constant's invention became emblematic for various facets of counterculture movements throughout Europe. Simultaneously in North America, counterculture movements were taking Canadian and American societies by storm. Having formed in the 1960s amidst the rise of counterculture in Toronto, the trio known as General Idea was key among artists' collectives promoting the total reconsideration of the social status quo. Made up of members Felix Partz, Jorge Zontal, and AA Bronson (all pseudonyms), the group was active from 1967 to 1994 and created films, made performances, staged raucous events, and generally poked fun at the perceived "normalcy" of the world around them, as evidenced in popular and media culture. In 1977 the trio produced a thirty-minute broadcast for Toronto's local television network in which they presented an extensive overview of their work. In doing so, they made clever use of television conventions, positioning the video somewhere between an educational program and news show. The viewer was no doubt left wondering whether or not to take it seriously, and

5 GENERAL IDEA
File Megazine, Vol. 5, no. 4 (1983), offset, 35.5 × 27.3 cm

6 GENERAL IDEA
File Megazine, Vol. 6, no. 1–2 (1984), offset, 35.5 × 27.3 cm

that was of course precisely the intention. What is authentic, and what is merely image? Thus General Idea succeeded in simultaneously creating a retrospective of their work – albeit with a highly "campy" caliber – while delivering an edgy and humorous commentary on mass media and the role of the artist in society. In the early 1980s, the trio launched *FILE Megazine*, which besides appropriating the typography used for *Life* magazine, most often depicted absurd photos on the covers which parodied the perceived seriousness of staged photography (fig. 5 and 6).
The emergence of counterculture as an ideology of revolution helped to form the basis of some of the most radical, absurd, and revolutionary art forms emerging in Europe and North America in the 1960s and '70s. Viewed through the perspective of creative practices, these objects illustrate the aesthetic push towards revolutionized chaos rather than passive acceptance, and the possibility of upheaval, even in the face of standardization.

8

VISIONARIES AND ACTIVISTS

1 KAZIMIR MALEVICH
Supremus no. 50, 1915, oil on canvas, 97.6 × 66.8 cm

VISIONAIRIES AND ACTIVISTS: ART FOR A NEW WORLD

Although much of the art produced during the late nineteenth and into the twentieth century bears witness to the struggle of artists to achieve more autonomy – to get away from the rules of art set by the academies, as well as to be free of commissioners, whether it be the church, the state, or private collectors – many avant-garde movements were nevertheless dedicated to an art that plays an important role in society. Art for art's sake was not a primary goal for many of the vanguard art movements of the twentieth century. Much more often they had a vision of the future and thought of their art as a – or rather, *the* – way to get there.

For example, around 1917, the time of the Russian Revolution, painter Kazimir Malevich and his fellow artists of the Russian avant-garde were convinced their art was the art of a new era. Colors and shapes speak their own language in suprematism, the expression of Malevich's belief that everything is in motion. Suprematist compositions depict the dynamics of planets, squirming bacteria, the living and not living, and visible and invisible nature in "pure" color and form. Malevich believed that this pure, painterly language would be timeless (fig. 1). Furthermore, he envisioned that suprematism could encompass all aspects of modern life, and broadened his scope to architecture and design. He designed, for instance, a number of "planits," or "future houses for

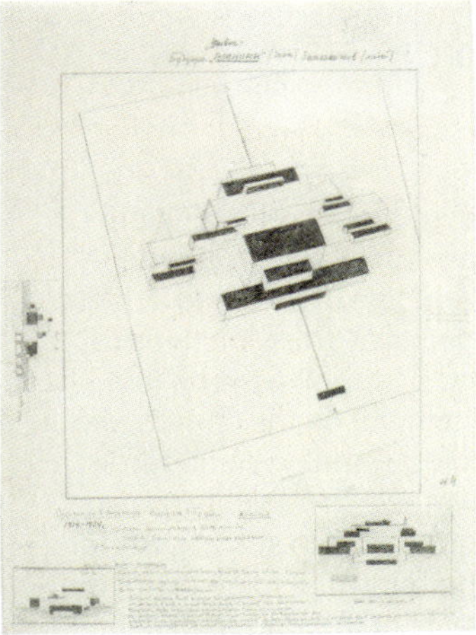

2 KAZIMIR MALEVICH
Toekomstige planits, huizen voor aardbewoners (The Houses of the Future), 1923, pencil on paper, 39 × 29.5 cm

3 THEO VAN DOESBURG AND CORNELIS VAN EESTEREN,
Contra-construction, presumably 1925, gouache and pencil on paper, 56.5 × 56.5 cm

inhabitants of the Earth" (fig. 2). The fact that his designs were far from practical and, quite frankly, unrealizable, did not dishearten Malevich, who was convinced technical difficulties would quickly become a matter of the past. After all, an artist shapes not the now, but the future. In a similar fashion and around the same time, the Dutch movement De Stijl wanted to contribute towards the shaping of this contemporary world. The future as envisioned by the artists of De Stijl was dynamic, energetic, colorful, and balanced. Art, design, and architecture should unite and strive towards harmony. This is beautifully expressed in the architectural models of Theo van Doesburg and architect Cornelis van Eesteren (fig. 3). Based on planes floating in space with the non-colors white, gray, and black, together with the three primaries of red, yellow, and blue, Van Doesburg and Van Eesteren conceived of the house as an open space that encompasses inside and out, while painting was not limited to a decorative role and instead gave dynamic impetus to the space. The conviction that unity between art, design, and architecture was paramount in creating art, and that design that could meet the demands of the technological society rapidly developing in the first half of the twentieth century, was also at the heart of the curriculum of the Bauhaus. Its founder, the German architect Walter Gropius, saw the school as "a cathedral of the future," where art and design would be united in order to create useful and beautiful objects fit for everyday life in a modern world (fig. 4).
The Second World War dealt a massive blow to artistic utopian visions of the future. Artists

4 MARCEL BREUER
Club Chair (model B3), also known as *Wassily Chair*,
design 1925-1928, manufactured presumably by Thonet Gebr. GmbH,
Frankenberg (DE), chrome plated steel, canvas, 75.5 × 77 × 68 × 40 cm

5 CONSTANT
Barricade, 1949, paint on canvas, 378.3 × 301.5 cm

attempted to reestablish identity and cope with the trauma of the war. One of these artists was Constant Nieuwenhuys, co-founder of the Dutch Cobra group in the late 1940s. In the years following the war, Constant engaged with its atrocities in his paintings, depicting concentration camps, death, and destruction in the typical bold and expressionist style of the Cobra group (fig. 5). Realizing, however, how automation was increasingly changing society, in 1956 Constant abandoned painting and started working on a visionary architectural proposal for a future society, titled New Babylon. Constant imagined a world without borders or constraints, where people would no longer need to work and would be free to play and travel at will: the *homo ludens* (man at play).

Yet, by the late 1950s and early '60s, a "cultural revolution" was underway, led by activists, thinkers, and artists who sought to rethink and even overturn what was, in their eyes, a stifling social order ruled by conformity. The Vietnam War incited mass protests in the United States, student protests in Paris signaled chaotic and revolutionary times in Europe, and the women's liberation movement gained momentum. Martha Rosler was and is one of those artists who critically engages with politics, mass media, and power relations within the art world, calling attention to power structures that oppress women. In the 1970s she eschewed the traditionally male-dominated art forms of painting and sculpture, instead choosing to work with media such as photography, video, and performance. Her film, *Semiotics of the Kitchen*, is a razor-sharp parody of a

6 MARTHA ROSLER
Semiotics of the Kitchen, 1975, video, black and white, sound,
6 min., 9 sec.

television cooking program (TV chef Julia Childs was incredibly popular in the 1970s). Rosler subverts the format of popular television cooking shows, which have changed little over the years (fig. 6). In an unremarkable kitchen, Rosler picks up cooking implements, systematically going through the alphabet, from apron to tenderizer. Her face remains expressionless, but her fierce gestures transform the innocent kitchenware items into potentially deadly weapons.

In the last decade nothing has appeared as urgently in the landscape of social critique as the topic of migration. Concerning both elective immigration as well as forced migration, the resulting clashing of cultures and reconsideration of national borders emerges frequently in the investigations of contemporary artists. For instance, Indian artist Nalini Malani focuses on the questionable nature of Indian identity when considered under the conditions of the migratory and problematic political foundations of its formation. In her work *Transgressions*, an installation she terms a "video/shadow play," the artist directs her attention towards the violence resulting from the 1947 Partition of India and Pakistan, combining mythological, Hindu, and historical narratives to confront the colonial, religious, and turbulent means by which the India of today continues to evolve (fig. 7).

7 NALINI MALANI
Transgressions, 2000, installation with video projection, color, sound, 6 min., 51 sec., mixed media, dimensions vary with installation

9 THE ROLE OF THE VIEWER

BETWEEN OBSERVATION AND EXPERIENCE: THE ROLE OF THE VIEWER

All art produces what is known as "experience." From the slightest change in attitude to being genuinely moved, artworks, like all visual materials, have an effect on our state of being when we look at them. For a long time the key words for this experience were peace and contemplation: standing quietly in front of a painting mounted on a white wall or slowly circling a sculpture opened the viewer to this experience. Even now, this is how we usually experience art. But that does not mean artists in the twentieth and twenty-first centuries have not done their best to throw these conditions in disarray. Not only have artists thoroughly questioned the shape and form of the artwork itself (see "Where did the art go?," pp. 351-361), but the viewer has often been assigned a radically different role as well. From a relatively static phenomenon, art transformed into a live act, whether in a performance, a happening, a gesture, or an action, in which the presence and participation of the public is essential. Though emerging most concretely in postwar Europe and the United States, the induction of performances and experience-based artworks did not appear without warning. Rather, various activities of the modern period can be viewed as having prefaced this later, more popular trend. One of the first sites of performance art was the highly political and often absurd activities of the Dada movement. In 1923 the Dutch

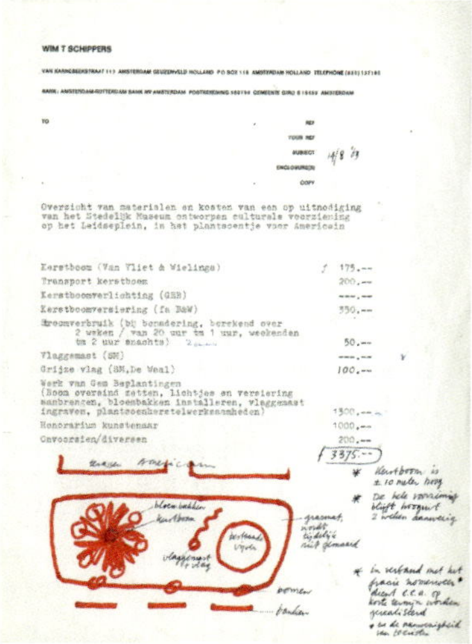

WIM T SCHIPPERS

TO

REF

YOUR REF

SUBJECT 14/8 '69

ENCLOSURE(S)

COPY

Overzicht van materialen en kosten van een op uitnodiging van het Stedelijk Museum ontworpen culturele voorziening op het Leidseplein, in het plantsoentje voor Americain

Kerstboom (Van Vliet & Wielinga)	ƒ 175.--
Transport kerstboom	200.--
Kerstboomverlichting (GEB)	---.--
Kerstboomversiering (fa B&W)	350.--
Stroomverbruik (bij benadering, berekend over 2 weken / van 20 uur tm 1 uur, weekenden tm 2 uur snachts)	50.--
Vlaggemast (SM)	---.--
Grijze vlag (SM, De Waal)	100.--
Werk van Gem Beplantingen (Boom overeind zetten, lichtjes en versiering aanbrengen, bloembakken installeren, vlaggemast ingraven, plantsoenherstelwerkzaamheden)	1300.--
Honorarium kunstenaar	1000.--
Onvoorzien/diversen	200.--
	ƒ 3375.--

* Kerstboom is ± 10 meter hoog

* De hele voorziening blijft hooguit 2 weken aanwezig

1 THEO VAN DOESBURG, possibly in collaboration with Kurt Schwitters
Kleine Dadasoirée (Little Dada Evening), 1922, lithograph, 30.1 × 30.7 cm

2 WIM T. SCHIPPERS
Letter and photo, 1969, 29.7 × 21 cm

avant-gardist Theo van Doesburg organized a "Dada campaign": a series of Dada evenings with mock lectures interrupted by barking audience members, absurd sketches, abstract poetry, and experimental music. Van Doesburg's poster design for the announcement of the evenings (fig. 1) shows a jumble of words in which the word "Dada" is repeated in bold letters. Slogans in French and German proclaim, "Dada is against the future, Dada is dead, Dada is idiotic, long live Dada!" These wild, unpredictable nights in front of a live audience, mixing visual arts, music, dance, and poetry, can be seen as setting the stage for artists looking for alternative strategies in the following decades. In the 1960s art increasingly began to exist outside of artists' studios, museums, and galleries. The happenings and performances by Fluxus, ZERO, and the nouveau réalistes were designed, in the spirit of Dada, to confuse and confound the audience; to insert art into everyday life. Passersby on Amsterdam's Leidse Square must have been quite surprised to encounter a very large Christmas tree, erected by Dutch Fluxus artist Wim T. Schippers in the middle of August 1969 (fig. 2). But performance increasingly became a medium for – at times very intense – explorations of social conventions and the relationship between the body and structures of power. In Valie Export's *TAPP- und TASTKINO* (*Tap and Touch Cinema*) (fig. 3) the audience did not get away with just watching; Export took her artwork into the street, inviting passersby to put their hands in a box with little curtains and join the "show" underneath – her naked body – for a maximum of thirty seconds. And in their

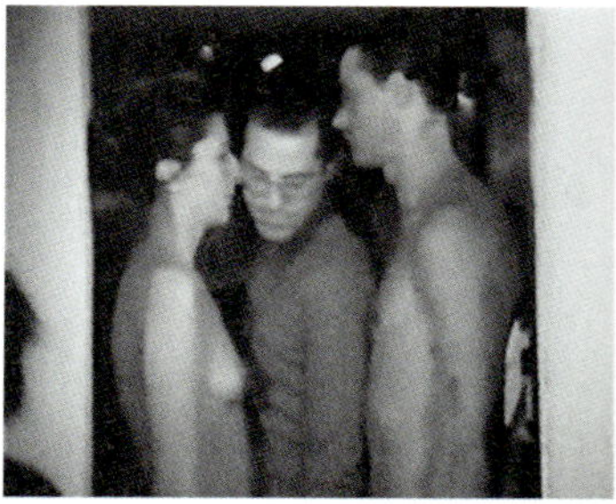

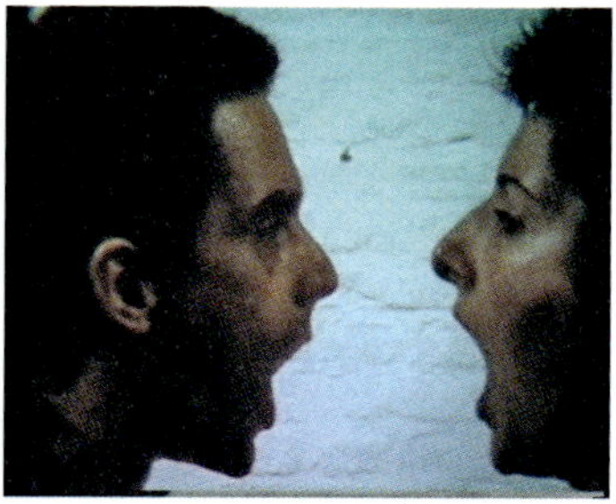

3 VALIE EXPORT
TAPP und TASTKINO, 1968/1969, video, b/w, sound, 1 min., 11 sec.

4 ULAY AND MARINA ABROMOVIĆ
Imponderabilia, 1977, video performance, b/w, sound, 9 min., 53 sec.

5 ULAY AND MARINA ABROMOVIĆ
AAA-AAA, 1978, video performance, color, sound, 20 min.

performance *Imponderabilia* by Ulay and Marina Abramović, the artists each stood naked the main entrance of the museum, forcing the public to choose which one of them to face (fig. 4).
Upon the invention of better filmic and photographic technologies, the documentation of performances began to stand in for the performances themselves, as otherwise a performance would be lost to the art world save for the select original viewers. Over time the documentation of performances evolved to the extent that performances were left with no viewers at all and were executed even for the very purpose of documentation. Famous for their aggressive bodily performances throughout the 1970s, the performances of Abramović and Ulay, for example, can be found in the museum's collection today in the form of black-and-white video documentation in which no viewers are represented. In one particular video, entitled *AAA-AAA* (fig. 5), the artists face one another with only centimeters between them, aggressively shouting "Ahhhh!" in the other's face. What is striking about the documentation of this performance is that it is a close-up shot of the artists' faces in profile, framing their open mouths in a way that the limited space between and loud noise they make become the focus of attention. This framing enhances the intensity of the performance, rendering the experience difficult to watch, even through the more "detached" medium of video. Because of this cinematic decision we see that the video of this performance was not for the sake of merely "documenting" what happened, but was directed towards the future viewer of the video, illustrating a consciousness

6 MARTIJN VAN NIEUWENHUYZEN
Audience at a performance by Tino Sehgal,
Stedelijk Museum Amsterdam, 2015

that the video itself would eventually stand in for the artwork when it came to the work being acquired by an art institution.
Performance and experience-based art remains a highly significant medium even today. In 2015, for instance, the Stedelijk Museum staged *A year at the Stedelijk: Tino Sehgal*, in which "situations," as the contemporary British-German artist describes his work, composed by Sehgal would take place at the museum, in the galleries themselves, each day for 365 days in a row. Sehgal's situations turn viewers into participants. Many of the titles of his works start with "this," in reference to the shared moment between performer and visitor. Sehgal sets the rules, but the elaboration depends on the visitor's reaction. In the work *This is Exchange*, for instance, visitors could earn two euros by engaging in a conversation on economics with a museum guard. In reality these guards were economists, hired by the museum as performers of Sehgal's piece. Unlike the documentary-based performances of the 1970s and '80s, Sehgal avoids any documentation of his projects. They only exist in a specific place, at a specific moment, exclusively for the people who are present (fig. 6). Upon a museum's acquisition of his work, Sehgal leaves no instructions and no available photographs, only his provision of those who can properly carry out the choreography and conditions for the pay and working conditions of the performers. In this way Sehgal aims to challenge the museum as a place of timeless preservation by creating a place in which the immediacy of contact, confrontation,

and experience can give way to a more political and discussion-based understanding of the institution.
To a certain extent, all art is performative. Something must be performed, in any case, for it to be made. The emergence of attention towards "experiential" art in the twentieth century, however, signaled a turn towards an artistic trend in which the subject no longer passively "receives" the work, but must be present in order for the work to function in the first place. From passivity to activity, the notion of the "experience" has transformed the relationship between viewer and artwork.

PHOTOGRAPHY AND DESIGN

10

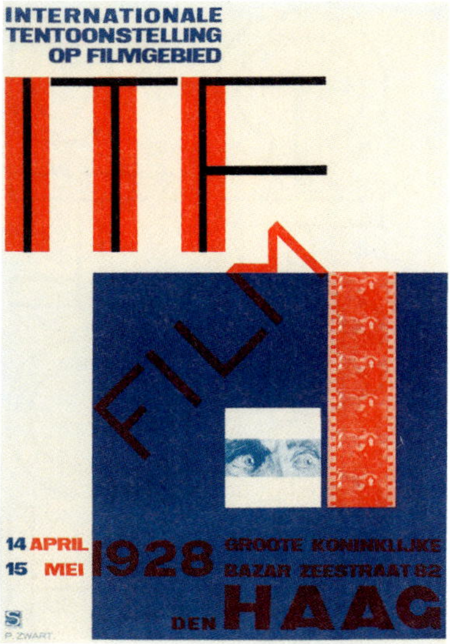

1 PIET ZWART
ITF Internationale tentoonstelling op filmgebied, 1928, printed by N.V. v/h J. Strang & Co's Drukkerijen, The Hague (NL), poster, offset, 86.2 × 61.1 cm

PHOTOGRAPHY AND DESIGN: THE URGE TO INNOVATE, ENGAGEMENT, AND AUTONOMY

Museums entirely devoted to photography and modern design are no exception these days. Photography and design also feature prominently in the Stedelijk Museum's collection. During the course of the twentieth century, these disciplines outgrew the "applied arts" label that had long been assigned to them.
In the nineteenth century photography initially depended in a formal sense on painting, though at the same time it developed numerous applications that focused on its qualities as a recording medium. Until the late nineteenth century, design was above all a craft. The progress of these disciplines towards their current status was a long process, defined to a large extent by the efforts of photographers and designers keen to exploit the technical and visual potential of their "medium," rather than simply using it to serve practical ends. The 1920s saw a broad change in direction in artistic terms, led by graphic designers, photographers, and designers. They were driven by political engagement and inspired by contemporary techniques and radical ideas about the relationship between art and society, like those put forward by De Stijl, Dada, and the Russian avant-garde. Dutch graphic designers Paul Schuitema and Piet Zwart, for example, were in close contact with the international avant-garde of the 1920s, and often used photographs in their cutting-edge designs (fig. 1). For them,

2 GERRIT RIETVELD
Birza Chair, 1927, bent fiber, fixed with bolt and nuts, 71.5 × 75 × 61 cm

3 KITTY VAN DER MIJLL DEKKER
Relief Rug, 1934, hand woven and knitted wool, 299 × 187 cm

photography was “technically the most perfect visual element and a fully-fledged visual means of expression.” Working as lecturers on the advertising course launched by the Royal Academy of Art, The Hague, in 1930, they trained a new generation of graphic designers and photographers. Among their students was Emmy Andriesse, who later became a reportage photographer. In the periods before, during, and after the Second World War, they produced work that combined the formal language of “New Photography” with social engagement (see p. 65).

Gerrit Rietveld, a member of the De Stijl movement, was also long concerned with finding ways of exploiting new technological potential. In 1927, for example, he designed the first chair that could be made from a single piece of material. The *Birza Chair* was a one-off (fig. 2), but the famous *Aluminum Chair* he designed during the war was intended to be made from plastic, emerging from a machine in a single piece, making it affordable to more families. The German Bauhaus also firmly believed that the application of new materials and techniques could help forge a new society. The Bauhaus was popular with women who, despite the high ideals of equality between the sexes, often ended up in the weaving workshop, like Dutch designer Kitty van der Mijll Dekker. The patterns in her trailblazing designs are not the result of using variously colored yarns, but of different knotting and weaving techniques—typical of the Bauhaus—as seen in her *Relief Rug* of 1934 (fig. 3).

Until the mid-twentieth century, applied or decorative art and photography were closely related,

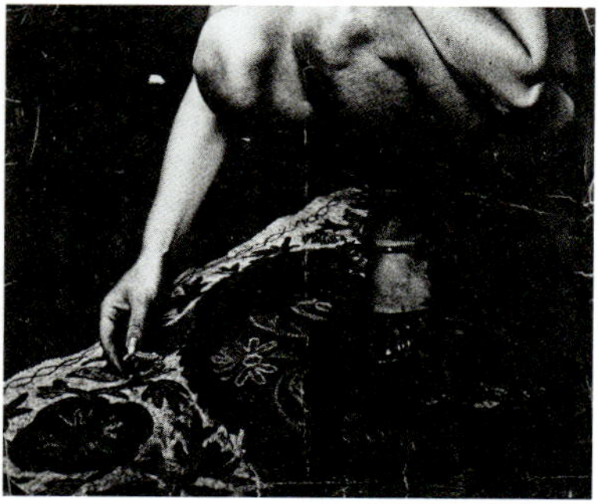

4 GERARD FIERET
Untitled, 1965–1975, gelatin silver print, 49.5 × 59.5 cm

5 ALVAR AALTO
(model 31/42), 1931–1932, production 1935–1940, manufactured by Artek Oy, Helsinki (FL), laminated birch frame, plywood seat and backrest veneered with Karelian birch, 68.9 × 61 × 71 cm

6 SHEILA HICKS
Trapèze de Cristobal (Trapeze of Cristobal), 1971, wool, linen, cotton, height variable, Ø 200 cm

and professional practitioners of these two disciplines in the Netherlands were initially members of the same association. This changed after the war. A new generation of photographers rejected the notion that photography was exclusively reliant on commissions. The young Ed van der Elsken showed, in his groundbreaking photonovel *Love on the Left Bank*, that photography could be a personal and expressive medium (see p. 77). This trend continued in the 1960s with the likes of Sanne Sannes and Gerard Fieret (fig. 4).
In modern design, social and artistic ideals retained their meaning. During the postwar reconstruction period, Dutch designers were strongly influenced by Scandinavian design. From about 1930, designers there had used wood (including curved wood) in combination with shapes, colors, and decoration drawn from nature to produce a softer and more human version of the taut lines, geometric forms, and primary colors of prewar modernism (fig. 5). The goal was to make attractive yet practical design available to all. Between 1950 and 1975, as the Netherlands underwent rapid industrialization and the country transformed into a modern welfare state, the position of "crafts" in relation to industry became a subject of debate. Ceramicists and textile and glass artists started making "autonomous" objects, and often had strong ties with the art world. This included Sheila Hicks and the duo of Gijs Bakker and Emmy van Leersum (p. 167). The interplay of colors, lines, and textures in Hicks's *Trapèze de Cristobal* reveals the influence of the Bauhaus, though the piece also claims the space in the manner of a sculpture (fig. 6).

7 KOEN WESSING
Santiago, 1973, gelatin silver print, 25.1 × 36.7 cm

8 ALFREDO JAAR
From the series *Faces*, 1982, chromogenic color print, 48.3 × 71.1 cm

Generally speaking, the dividing lines between design, photography, and fine art were becoming increasingly blurred, while at the same time many forms of exchange and mutual influence could also be discerned. The use of photography in conceptual art (see, for example, Jan Dibbets, p. 177) and the critical use of the medium led to radical new forms of photography in the 1970s and '80s, like the work of the Picture Generation, which included Cindy Sherman (p. 205). Artists also manifested their photographic engagement in new ways. This included Chilean artist Alfredo Jaar, who was inspired by Koen Wessing's images of the Chilean coup d'état in the early 1970s (figs. 7 and 8).

There is more autonomy in design, too, probably partly as a result of the fact that many designers now train at art academies. This can be seen, for example, in the work of Gert Dumbar and Mevis & Van Deursen. The latter, in particular, produce striking, conceptually oriented designs that go further than merely communicating a specific message as simply as possible, with explicit additional visual qualities that enhance the commission (figs. 9 and 10). Dutch Design, which emerged in the 1990s, is also closely associated with a conceptual and/or narrative content, as seen in the work of Marcel Wanders and Wieki Somers (p. 253).

Since the late twentieth century there has also been a reappraisal of crafts, craftsmanship, and handiwork in relation to technology and industry. The same applies to graphic design, where "traditional" techniques like screen printing, stenciling and Risograph printing have recently attracted

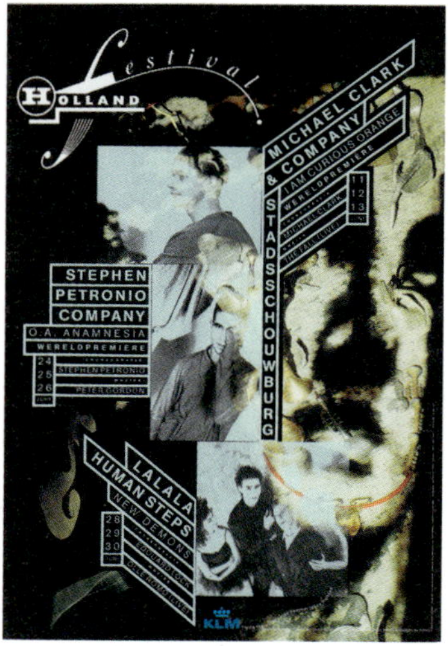

9 STUDIO DUMBAR
Holland Festival Stadsschouwburg, 1988, screenprint, 117.8 × 82.8 cm

10 MEVIS EN VAN DEURSEN
Sabotage Baby, 2000, screenprint, 118.2 × 84.2 cm

11 OLIVIER VAN HERPT
Object 4: Organic, Object 8: Organic, Object 5: Organic, 2016, 3D printed ceramics, h. 47 × Ø 32.5 cm, h. 18, Ø 50.5 cm, h. 81.5, Ø 25 cm

renewed interest. The boundaries between industrial design and applied art are becoming increasingly blurred. Olivier Van Herpt, for example, uses a 3D printer as a kind of extension of his hand to make complex ceramic vases (fig. 11). This is not a question of mass production, but of complete control over the entire production process, from programming to execution to finished product. The dominant "trend" in design is extensive material research to identify alternative, sustainable raw materials, as well as a rejection of mass production and consumption. Designers are seeking both high- and low-tech ways of rediscovering the materials and elements they work with and using them in innovative ways. Materials are derived from waste, recycled and upcycled to revive their texture, form, and color. One good example is the work of Christien Meindertsma (p. 251). Social engagement also plays a key role. Design duo Metahaven, for example, created a series of T-shirts and large silk scarves for the controversial journalism platform WikiLeaks. These can cover the body and face of the wearer, but are at the same time translucent (fig. 12). The designs refer to the ambiguity of WikiLeaks, a platform that strives for transparency, even while its sources, administrators, and procedures are shrouded in secrecy. The profits from the sale of these items helped WikiLeaks in its battle for survival.

In the 1990s there was a reappraisal of the value of unmanipulated, immediate images, as seen in the work of Rineke Dijkstra (p. 227), who, like many other photographers, also branched out into video art. Autonomy and engagement are

12 METAHAVEN
Transparent Camouflage, 2011–2013/2016, mixed media, various dimensions

13 ZANELE MUHOLI
Bester I, Mayotte (Hail the Dark Lioness), from the series *Somnyama Ngonyama*, gelatin silver print, 60.5 × 80.5 cm

essential to contemporary work, as evidenced by the intense images by Dana Lixenberg and the confrontational self-portraits by South African photographer Zanele Muholi (fig. 13).

INDEX A–M

EXTENDED CAPTIONS FOR THE ESSAYS

p. 294 (fig. 2) Gift of the Vereniging Vrienden van Vincent van Gogh en zijn tijd, 1942
p. 294 (fig. 3) Gift of the heirs of Mrs. Jenny van Leeuwen-Lütens, Amsterdam (NL), 1955
p. 294 (fig. 4) Acquired with the generous support of the Vereniging Rembrandt, Theo van Gogh Stichting and NN, 1975
p. 296 (fig. 7) Purchased with the generous support of the VVHK, 1962
p. 298 (fig. 9) Gift of the VVHK, 1949
p. 306 (fig. 2) Bequeathed by Helge Spechter-Höxbroe, Amsterdam (NL), 1963
p. 310 (fig. 6) Gift of The Mark Rothko Foundation, Inc. through The American Federation
of Arts, New York (US), 1986
p. 312 (fig. 8) Gift of the Stichting Vrienden van het Stedelijk Museum, 2014
p. 318 (fig. 4) Ownership recognized by agreement with the estate of Kazimir Malevich in 2008
p. 322 (fig. 8) Gift of Mrs. Barnett Newman in Honor of Edy de Wilde, Director of the Stedelijk Museum Amsterdam 1963-1984, 1992
p. 324 (fig. 9) Gift of Sol LeWitt and Carl Andre, 2003
p. 334 (fig. 5) Acquired with the generous support of the Stichting Vrienden van het Stedelijk Museum, 1999
p. 336 Gift of Museum De Paviljoens, Almere (NL), 2015
p. 340 (fig. 2) Gift of Martijn en Jeannette Sanders, 2015
p. 342 Gift of Mrs. Katherine S. Dreier, USA, 1949
p. 348 (fig. 8) Gift of the artist, 2010
p. 376 and 378 (fig. 2) Ownership recognized by agreement with the estate of Kazimir Malevich in 2008
p. 380 (fig. 5) Gift of the artist, 1970
p. 384 Acquired with the generous support of the Mondriaan Fund, 2002
p. 392 (fig. 5) Gift of NN, 1978
p. 402 (fig. 3) Gift of the VANK, 1935
p. 406 (fig. 7) Long-term loan from the Cultural Heritage Agency of the Netherlands
p. 406 (fig. 8) Acquired with the generous support of the Mondriaan Fund, 2014

CREDITS

IMAGE CREDITS

The copyright for all images used lies with the artist, unless specified otherwise in the list below. For works of visual artists affiliated with CISAC-organisation the copyrights have been settled with Pictoright in Amsterdam. © 2017, c/o Pictoright, Amsterdam

pp. 48-50, 296, 320 © 2012 Mondrian/ Holtzman Trust c/o HCR International USA
p. 52 Eva Besnyö/MAI
p. 62 Erven Sandberg (c/o Halinka Augustin, openoog@luna.nl)
p. 64 c/o Joost Elffers 2017/ Stedelijk Museum Amsterdam
pp. 76, 280 (1962, top left) © Photo Museum Rotterdam, collection Ed van der Elsken estate
pp. 82-84 Succession Henri Matisse
p. 120 © The Willem de Kooning Foundation 2017
p. 134 © 2017 Estate of Edward Kienholz
pp. 170, 358 courtesy Egress Foundation
p. 188 © The Estate of Philip Guston, courtesy Hauser & Wirth
p. 200 © 2017 Dara Birnbaum. Courtesy Electronic Arts Intermix (EAI), New York
p. 204 Courtesy of Cindy Sherman en Metro Pictures, New York
p. 208 © Nan Goldin, courtesy Matthew Marks Gallery
pp. 210, 284 (1986) © The Keith Haring Foundation 2017
p. 212 © Estate Martin Kippenberger, courtesy Galerie Gisela Capitain, Cologne
p. 214 © Steven Flavin/Artists Rights Society (ARS), New York, courtesy David Zwirner, New York
pp. 220, 300 (fig. 10) © 2017 Judd Foundation/Artists Rights Society (ARS), New York
p. 230 © Gilbert & George, courtesy White Cube
pp. 238-240 © Grayson Perry en Victoria Miro Gallery
p. 264 © Isa Genzken/Courtesy Galerie Buchholz, Berlin/Cologne
p. 406 (fig. 7) © Koen Wessing/Hollandse Hoogte

PHOTO CREDITS

All photographs © Stedelijk Museum Amsterdam, unless otherwise specified
Photography pp. 32-33, 72-72, 82-82, 86-87, 94-95, 98-99, 104-105, 122-123, 152-153, 158, 174-175, 180, 216-217, 232-233, 238-239, 242-243, 244, 256-257, 260, 262, 264, 268, 288 (2007) Gert Jan van Rooij
p. 274 (1894) Jacob Olie, © City Archives Amsterdam
p. 280 (1969) © Ad Petersen
p. 288 (2012) © John Lewis Marshall

The Stedelijk Museum made every effort to find the copyright holders for the illustrations used. Interested parties are requested to contact the Stedelijk Museum Amsterdam, Van Baerlestraat 31, 1071 AN, Amsterdam.

Concept and
Compilation
Sophie Tates

With texts by
Megan Mullarky, Sophie Tates,
Hanneke de Man

Text editing
Mariëtte Wijne

Copyediting
Dutton Hauhart – Reitz Ink

Translation
Dutch – English
Sue McDonnell

Project Management
Sabien Stols

Project Assistance
Alie Sonneveldt, Katie Wolters

Thanks to
Karin Balog, Eva Heisterkamp,
Sarah Knigge, Gert-Jan van Rooij,
Margriet Schavemaker,
Hetty Wessels, Hripsimé Visser,
Martijn van Nieuwenhuyzen

Layout & Design
Meeusontwerpt

Lithography & Print
Graphius – Belgium

Binding
Binderij Hexspoor bv, Boxtel

ISBN 978 90 5006 199 5

Stedelijk cat. no. 938

Stedelijk Museum is supported by:

Gemeente Amsterdam

Principal sponsor

Rabobank

Partner

BankGiro Loterij

WWW.STEDELIJK.NL